STYLE BY SALADINO

ST_{BY}YLE
SALADINO

John F. Saladino

PRINCIPAL
PHOTOGRAPHY BY
BARBARA AND
RENÉ STOELTIE

THE MONACELLI PRESS

This book is dedicated to Graham and Kristen,
my son and his wife
VI.XXIV.MM

First published in the United States of America in 2000
by The Monacelli Press, Inc.
10 East 92nd Street,
New York, New York, 10128

STYLE BY SALADINO
Copyright © 2000 Frances Lincoln Limited
Text copyright © 2000 John F. Saladino
Photographs copyright © 2000 Barbara and René Stoeltie except those listed on page 208

First Frances Lincoln edition: October 2000

Library of Congress Catalog Card Number: 00-106587

ISBN: 1-58093-080-8

STYLE BY SALADINO was edited, designed, and produced by Frances Lincoln Ltd., London

Printed and bound in Hong Kong

PAGE 1 I have been caught in
a reflective mood by a mirror,
which has been reflecting images
for four hundred years, in the
apartment seen on pages 132-5.
PREVIOUS PAGES, THIS PAGE AND
OPPOSITE The dining room and
hallway of the apartment seen on
pages 188-203.

CONTENTS

PREFACE

I BELIEVE that our surroundings have a profound effect on us. At their most sublime they can move us, take us out of this world, and give us what I call "moments of transcendence."

When I was growing up in Kansas City, Missouri, I often traveled on a bus across town to the Nelson Gallery of Art at weekends. I realize now that I was going there primarily not so much for the works of art themselves, but for the effect that the interiors had on me. I loved the great black marble-columned, four-story-high entrance hall, the austerity of the Egyptian gallery with its heads of Rameses and Anubis, the haunting medieval cloister, the rich Cromwellian room, and the light-flooded Italian stone court

with its marble benches and pots of oleander. The feeling of transcendence, of serenity and—paradoxically—of homecoming that was engendered by those spaces shaped my vision. Now, when I am designing, I return again and again to the lessons that I learned from them.

Over the years, there have been several places in which I have felt a similar mix of emotions. Living in Rome as a young man I remember the exhilaration of standing in the Pantheon as the light streamed in through the oculus above me. A few years later, when I walked through Rameses's hall in Luxor (*left*), even though the roof was missing the effect of the columns, which are 80 feet high and so vast at the base that it takes five men with arms outstretched to encircle one, swept me off my feet, elevating me from my own physicality. But perhaps the most memorable moment of all was my visit to the studio of the sculptor Brancusi (*right*). When I stepped

inside I immediately became part of a reality totally different from any that existed in the outside world—an emotional experience similar to being engulfed by a great opera or symphony. Surrounding me in the tall room were the collected works of a genius, their effect all the more powerful for being seen together. Sleekly polished bronzes and gleaming marbles were balanced on crude bases made from wine tourniquets. The objects in the room were covered with white marble dust and the light filtering down from the frosted glass ceiling veiled everything below in an even luminescence. I had walked into not just a room, but a work of art. I understood all at once why Brancusi always wore white clothes, why he wore that

funny little hat straight out of *I Pagliacci*, and why his white dog drank milk and ate pale lettuce. I felt as though I had become part of the still life.

Standing there taught me that art can be not just something hung on the wall or put on a pedestal—it can be all-encompassing, and a whole room can have as powerful an emotional effect as any work of art. It was an extraordinarily moving experience.

I felt a similar sensation when I first entered the gardens of the Villa d'Este at Tivoli, near Rome (*below*). For me, water is the single most important element in any garden: the combination of sound and movement as well as constantly changing visual interest brings a garden to life; and here I was surrounded by water that was spouting, gushing, spilling and cascading from an unimaginable number of jets and fountains, steps, pools, and grottoes. It had done so for four centuries, with the result that all the sculpted surfaces

were covered in a velvety green moss. This, in combination with the superbly articulated site and beautifully controlled vistas, each leading to another surprise or reward, made the experience almost hypnotic in its intensity.

On a more intimate scale, but with an atmosphere almost as seductive as the Villa d'Este, is the Crowninshield garden (*right*) on the old Du Pont estate in Wilmington, Delaware. Made in the 1930s to look like an Italian archeological site with fragments and statues brought to America from Europe, it is redolent of the faded grandeur of the Roman Empire, but exerts a spell that never loses its potency.

These early experiences demonstrate the immense influence that our environments exert on our senses. This is why I think that houses should cater to our emotional needs, and why I say to clients, "If you walk into a room and it does not move you, then the room is a failure."

The reason many people seek help in designing their interior space—aside from considerations of time—is, I believe, because we live in a world in which people are taught how to read and how to calculate, but are not taught how to see. "Learning to see" is not part of the educational curriculum. In contrast to the emphasis placed on developing quantitative skills, and even competence in some of the other arts such as literature, it seems to me that most students' visual education is left largely immature and unformed.

It is my wish to address this lack of visual skill, and to awaken an awareness of the potential for beauty in your surroundings, that prompted me to write this book. By presenting the keys to the door of my way of "seeing"—the principles and guidelines that frame my design thinking—I hope that you may be helped to develop your own powers of perception, and create an environment that will lift your spirits and nurture your soul.

GUIDING PRINCIPLES

EVERY HOME should be a sanctuary: entering it you should immediately feel physically and emotionally protected. Inside there should ideally be two different, but equally important, kinds of space that metaphorically might be described as a cocoon and a cathedral. We all need space that offers comfort and security, and shelter from the cold, noise or darkness outside. But, paradoxically, we also need space that liberates us from terra firma, allowing our spirits to soar and our imaginations to take flight.

All my work is based on this precept; it is the foundation stone of my design philosophy. It does not follow that only small rooms can be cocoons, or that only huge spaces can elicit a feeling of liberation. The opposite is often true: a tiny, exquisite bathroom can be as transcendent as the most glittering ballroom.

Before I have even begun to think about the design of a house or garden for clients, I ask them to bring me three lists—of "musts," "hates," and "maybes," and a box of "dreams." In this box I ask them to put visual references— magazine clippings, photos, books—of the things that they feel most passionate about. This box is as important to me as all the items on the three lists put together. Good design is about turning dreams into reality.

Design, like other art forms, depends on a sequence of calculated choices. The principles that guide my design choices can be traced to pivotal personal encounters—many of which date back to the time I spent in Italy as a young man.

I originally studied painting at the Yale School of Art and Architecture, then worked in various design studios in New York before spending two years in an architectural practice in Rome. Those years were seminal. I have often said that I am a romantic by nature, a minimalist by training, but by choice, a classicist. Rome released the romantic in me, freeing me from the inhibitions and guilt instilled in me by my catholic education, but did not suppress the minimalist. More importantly, it developed the classicist in me. Sometimes the debt to the classicism in my

LEFT The drawing room in my former New York apartment was originally a ballroom, but by zoning the space to make rooms within rooms, and by using high-backed sofas, I created intimate, cozy retreats.

LEFT Classic in its symmetrical setting, the bathroom I designed for a New York apartment would be almost spartan in its simplicity but for the luxurious quality of the materials that are used.

work is explicit, at other time it is implicit. But the influence is always present: in my linear thinking, in my love of simple shapes and symmetry, in my handling of scale, and in my obsession with light. The romantic side of my nature is perhaps most obvious in my infatuation with theatrical statements and illusion; but it is also evident in my deep attachment to our links with the past. Minimalism, the third influential strand in the plait of my work, is apparent in the strength of my urge to pare away unnecessary details, to edit my surroundings.

In the chapters that follow I explain how my guiding principles work in practice, illustrating them with examples from the houses and gardens that I have designed. Impossible to separate, because they pervade all aspects of my designs, are my predilections for classic shapes, for abstraction, and for allusions to the passage of time.

In understanding the power of shape and form, the seventeenth-century Dutch painter Vermeer is a model for me. He placed people and furnishings, windows and architecture, in the foreground of his canvases with such precision that he made still lifes of these elements. Taking lessons from his paintings, I challenge my clients to stop thinking about design as having to do with merchandise and furniture and, instead, hope that they will come to believe, as I do, that a room should be like a walk-in still life. By that I mean the space should demonstrate an orchestration of shapes in harmony with each other. At every step, decisions of shape and space must be made that will add or subtract from the overall design harmony: Is the chair beautiful to look at from the back as you walk into the room? Should it be open-backed because the room is small and you do not want it to steal space? Every decision narrows the options.

I see furnishings firstly as geometry—as squares, cubes, drums, triangles, and rectangles, which also happen to be sofas, chairs, tables, lamps, and paintings, and this is reflected in the designs for my own collection. I dislike most modern furniture for its discomfort,

vulgarity, and its short aesthetic shelf life, and always seek or try to design furniture that will not betray its age in ten or even thirty years.

An interior still life should be a room that is not only carefully furnished but also possibly even *under*-furnished. I like to think of a room as more closely resembling a drawing than a completed painting. In a drawing the possibility always exists of adding or erasing part of the design; and besides, drawings are often more exciting than paintings because they reveal the artist's thought processes.

One of the crucial roles of the designer and architect is to bring discipline and selectivity to bear, so that clients do not fill their houses all at once with everything that they own. We need to make our visual strainers finer and sift through the plethora of our possessions. After all, a discerning woman does not wear her all her jewelry at the same time.

Designing environments is about editing. Editing is critical to making beauty. In any design plan the objects excluded are every bit as significant as the objects included. Good decorating demands a developed sense of closure—like good tennis, you win with fewer strokes when you feel confident.

Vermeer also showed that there should be a happy marriage between positive and negative space. In other words, the space in a room should not be conceived as simply a vessel waiting to be filled —like the empty space between trees in a forest. In a successful design composition, the room has as much validity as the objects it holds. A wall, for example, can be a valid entity in itself rather than being merely the background and support for a picture.

The concept of being part of a continuum of time is important to me and a recurring theme in my work. Any fragments from the past, especially those that you can touch, connect you to the makers of those pieces, making you aware that we are threads in a great tapestry of time. Antique mirrors are perhaps the best example as they literally held images of the past—think of the people who have looked into them over the years. I also think of the craftsmen who made those mirrors. Mercury glazing was a dangerous occupation and early artisans gave their lives for their craft, dying young when the mercury infiltrated their bodies and poisoned them. Historically, mirrors have been so highly prized that it is not unusual to find European wills listing mirrors left in an estate even before the land.

For me, connecting with the past plays a prominent role in planning the restoration of, or an addition to, an old house. When my late wife and I had our first house, an eighteenth-century forge, it fell to us to add a kitchen. We used old wood, scratch-coat plaster, and wide oak floorboards, and we partly concealed the refrigerator and stove, so that the room resembled an old pantry with pieces of antique furniture along the wall. We were proud of the resulting effect and eager to show it to my parents who were visiting the house for the first time. When my mother walked into the kitchen there was a gasp, followed by, "Oh my God, it's going to cost you a fortune to rip out all this old wood."

OPPOSITE Hanging a triangular William and Mary walnut mirror on the wall above two Japanese storage chests in my son's room has made an abstract composition. RIGHT When friends asked me to help them renovate their seventeenth-century house, I halted the workmen who were stripping away the accreted layers of paint when they reached this stage. To me the original surfaces are a perfect homage to the first decorators.

Even when I am building or designing a modern house with twenty-first-century materials, I try to incorporate those that will age gracefully. For example, aluminum has the unattractive feature of developing pits as it grows old, whereas wood always looks wonderful. It is important to choose materials that will offset some of the newer technology and ensure the beauty that comes with passing time.

I like to think of an interior as incomplete, as a fragment of a time continuum. I have an abhorrence of everything being perfect; most modern homes seem too slick and shiny. This is why I often use materials not generally regarded as finished surfaces. I like the surfaces of corroded concrete, raw silk, weathered wood, and worn leather. I take inspiration from archaeological excavations where classical shards, surfaces, and fragments are strewn about. I may use a peeling wooden capital, rescued from a building scheduled to be demolished, as an overscale base for a hall table; or I might place a nearly threadbare chair in an entrance hall as a piece of sculpture. I do not often restore antiques— the old finish with its fading patina is what I am after.

In the same way, if a design is so programmed that it borders on being perfect I cannot resist denying that control by doing something that appears to be accidental or haphazard. For example, an overscale bedspread that drags on the floor will do a great deal to soften the lines of a too-glossy, cube-like room. Also, the simple act of leaning paintings or mirrors against a wall rather than hanging them,

especially in a crisply contemporary house, psychologically dilutes the intimidating effect of perfection, and makes the interior feel unfinished, as if it was awaiting the hand of time.

My strongly held belief that the house should be a sanctuary is echoed by my conviction that the garden should be a version of Arcadia, a place cut off from the rest of the world where dreams can be pursued. Like a house, a garden can evoke intense, heightened feelings. Even a single bloom can offer a vision of paradise. Think of those aristocrats of flowers, the 'Casablanca' lilies; in addition to their unrivaled beauty, they release their glorious scent when the sun sets, so that even in the dark they have a presence. Have you ever walked by orange trees in bloom or a hedge of star jasmine? The sensuality of this experience is far more intoxicating than any bottled scent.

The Italians have a saying, "We have a life of action so that we may inherit a life of serenity." I believe most people come to gardening later in life, either for the purely prosaic reason that that is when they move to a house with a garden, or because after years of struggling to make the world the way they want it—and realizing that it can never be—they turn to the garden in solace and use their energies to a make a world that is more manageable, and gather around them the plantings that support their inner vision.

In seeking to make my own visions of Arcadia in my

LEFT My version of Arcadia at Robin Hill, my house in Connecticut.
RIGHT The espaliered trees, clipped evergreens and beds of miniature gypsophylia make an abstract pattern of the garden nearest the house.

gardens in Connecticut and California, I have found that I have been inspired by the idealized landscapes painted by Poussin and Claude Lorrain, as well as some of the world's most celebrated classic gardens. You, too, are bound to be influenced by what you have seen. Never think that the spellbinding beauty of the greatest gardens is out of reach. Just as the value of paintings is not judged by dimensions or medium, nor music by how many instruments are used, your own Elysium has nothing to do with the size or shape of your property. Rather than attempting simply to copy something, try to analyze what it is that most appeals to you and distill that into your own personal statement.

In my view, architecture, interior design, and gardening are all part of the same intellectual process and subject to the same laws and aesthetic analysis, and similar principles govern my approach to planning a garden as guide my work on interiors. Axial planning, considerations of scale, use of illusion, dramatic light, and subtle color all come into play, as do my penchants for simple shapes and uncluttered lines and my feeling for timelessness.

There is, of course, one essential difference between decorating and gardening: the latter is a partnership with nature. You cannot control every detail of the outside environment in the same way as you can the inside. Gardens constantly shift and change—reminding us of the transitory nature of our own existence—and you are always at the mercy of the vagaries of the weather. Vita Sackville-West, one of the legendary creators of the gardens at Sissinghurst, Kent, said that to be a good gardener you have to be tenacious. With that I concur, but would add that you have also to be patient. It may take eight years to establish a garden that looks as though it did not just come out of the back of a station wagon after visiting a nursery. You can, however, imitate nature. Noticing how the wind scatters seeds and where birds drop them, I plant bulbs and flowers in clusters up against walls and rocks as though they had landed there by accident. And I plant mature bushes close to a terrace of a new house to give the illusion that it has been there a long time.

I often find that people fail to bring to their gardens the same seriousness that they bring to their houses: the sum that they are willing to spend on a single important carpet is sometimes the total budget for the entire garden, even though the garden is usually much bigger than the house. I always tell clients that in the making of a house or garden there is one thing you must do first: go out and buy the special work of art, or the spectacular mature tree, or the fifty rose bushes you have always craved. I agree with Frank Lloyd Wright's dictum: first buy the luxuries, the necessities will take care of themselves. At the end of a project, you will always find enough funds to buy the washer and the dryer but will forgo the antiques, the works of art, and the large shade tree. I believe that it is better to feed your soul from the beginning.

Another common failing is not to understand that the entire property is a garden. To clients who say, "We want to plant a garden in the yard," I explain that the yard *is* the garden! The notion that garden and yard are separate derives from the Victorian practice of making flower beds like carpets in which all the plants were subservient to a rigid geometry. Even the smallest lot is a canvas on which to create a picture and, like all good artists, gardeners must consider the whole as well as the particulars.

Looking at the particulars may require being strict with yourself, limiting your planting to what you can appropriately accommodate in the space. This is the equivalent to editing in the house. If you have always loved the practical side of gardens, such as fruit-bearing trees, but your property is tiny, you should choose two miniature apple trees in pots, or just one other fruit-bearing tree that will double as a shade tree. The same discipline is needed when ordering flowers from a catalogue. (I also find it wise to write down next to my choices the other flowers that I plan to plant beside them.)

In planning a garden I try to make sure that the part that is closest to the house is the most articulated and artificial. This is where I make the most use of manmade features and clipped and trained plants. In fact my two favorite garden activities are pruning and shaping. It is through these that the beauty of abstract form takes most obvious hold in the garden. But this is not to say that I want a garden full of parterres and mazes—when a garden becomes too artificial it is only about control. Don't forget that nature provides its own form of abstraction in the variety of shapes made by trees or shrubs. For planting further away from the house, choose a range of spreading, weeping, columnar, pyramidal, or fastigiate trees and shrubs, and plant them in groups to make the best contrasts.

Abstraction in the garden is not the prerogative of any one time of year. I find my garden at Robin Hill exquisite when blanketed by snow, when the shapes of the clipped shrubs and the wrapped objects become Christo sculptures and it becomes truly a walk-in still life.

Artifacts and fragments used outdoors bring mystery to the garden and, if they are old, a mingling of the past with the present. "Ruins" in the form of fallen columns or vine-covered follies are romantic ways to suggest that the garden has existed over time. A door in the middle of an old stucco wall that opens into a wild area suggests that earlier buildings had previously existed. Trees that were felled by storms and have regenerated are living fragments, trophies from the past that also lend mystery and maturity to the planting around them. In my garden in Connecticut I have a long narrow, very worn, veined-marble Roman sink resting on Baroque stone supports, and a second-century marble sarcophagus, both of which are seasonally planted. I have also re-created my own Roman "Appian Way"—200 feet of a new "ancient street." It is my interpretation of an eighteenth-century folly and lends a mysterious image of power and decay, suggestive of some vanished civilization, to the surroundings.

I paved this "street" in my garden at Robin Hill with enormous irregular flat stones, cut to order from local stone, on a 3-foot-high platform in the middle of a meadow. Small bulbs for the spring, dianthus, veronica with beautiful silver leaves and blue blossoms, and three kinds of thyme are planted between the stones.

AXIS

Corridors of desire

The enfilade through my house, Robin Hill, from the drawing room, through the octagonal entrance hall, to the breakfast room. The visual reward at the end is the octagonal silver and cobalt-blue glass lantern hanging above the breakfast table.

BELOW The path that takes visitors to the Villa Rotonda, near Vicenza, restricts the view on both sides so that it remains focused on the classical, colonnaded façade.

OPPOSITE Looking through the enfilade at the Villa Barbaro, near Vicenza, one sees Veronese's beckoning figure; he is the reward at the end of the visual journey. The villa was originally built as a summer residence, and beyond the first, outside, door, all the "woodwork" that surrounds the doors is *trompe l'oeil*.

I WAS NINETEEN when I first visited the Villa Rotonda, one of the sixteenth-century architect Palladio's most famous houses, in the environs of Vicenza. The day was gray and uninviting and, it not being the tourist season, everything was closed. To gain entry my brother and I resorted to using white envelopes containing whatever tips we could afford. The tactic finally succeeded and the gates were opened. In front of us stretched a straight path that led up a steep hill with only a small glimpse of the villa's entrance at the summit to lure us on. Starting at the bottom, we felt the exhilaration of anticipation as we climbed; stone walls on right and left were like horse blinders, screening out any distractions. At the top of the ascent we were rewarded by the sight of the whole, dazzlingly beautiful villa and its glorious 360-degree view.

Not far from the Villa Rotonda is the Villa Barbaro, which has a very different, but equally unforgettable, use of axis. The house, which was also designed by Palladio, is made up of a series of rooms with plastered walls but little or no woodwork. The flat walls are decorated with wonderful theatrical *trompe l'oeil* frescoes by the sixteenth-century master Veronese. Visitors are enticed through the rooms by these painted figures until they come to the enchanting, tongue-in-cheek reward—the illusion of a young man, the owner of the house, stepping out of a doorway to greet them.

One of the earliest and, to my mind one of the finest, Palladian houses to be built in the English-speaking world is Chiswick House, near London, with architecture by Lord Burlington, and interiors by William Kent. This eighteenth-century jewel is a masterpiece of axial planning. As you walk through the house, you move from darkness to light, from narrow enclosure to expansive space. The idea of creating a visual journey that draws you—or your eye—along, pricking curiosity, manipulating emotions, and increasing

RIGHT The chief enfilade at Chiswick House goes through the central rotunda and leads to a magnificent fireplace, framed by Corinthian columns. The apsial arch creates an area of darkness that dramatizes the light-filled room beyond.

OPPOSITE The view, which I devised, from the entrance hall to the dining room at a client's house, Las Tejas, in California, was based on my experience of Chiswick House. The pair of antique vases, illuminated by light sources hidden in the plinths below them, reinforces the symmetry.

anticipation until the reward is reached has been seminal in my work; and my designs are very involved with enfilade, with creating a visual corridor. I often recall the Arab proverb "Narrow is the passage to heaven" when I advise people who are decorating their own homes to keep in mind that the end of a visual journey, even if the journey is only a corridor, should have a completion, a reward. If it is not closed doors, then perhaps it could be a barometer, or a vase of beautifully arranged flowers.

My own house in Connecticut is based on a complex use of enfilade. The house can be thought of as a long train that has come to rest in the middle of a garden. In the middle of the train is an octagonal entrance hall with a weathered relic of an Italian stone wellhead as its centerpiece, breaking up the long axis that stretches from one end of the house to the other. This room also sits at the crossing of another axis, allowing anyone standing here to see in all four cardinal directions—an architectural idea emphasized by Palladio. All four vistas end in glass, with views to the garden.

Axis and enfilade play an important role in the so-called "Venetian" apartment that I created for clients in New York City. It illustrates my belief that we experience architecture sequentially. I devised an inner sanctum, a sequence of rooms— unified by a light palette—that open up into one another. First is an entrance foyer; here, to evoke the appearance of an outdoor space, the walls are finished in crude scratch-coat plaster and the floor is made of honed volcanic stone, which has been left unfilled. This room is where visitors leave the reality of New York City behind and pause before moving through an archway into the first reception room, which is a more refined, less textural space—an experience not unlike passing through the barnacled exterior of a shell into the smooth central interior.

BELOW The visual corridor in the New York "Venetian" apartment is clear from my sketch of the ground plan.

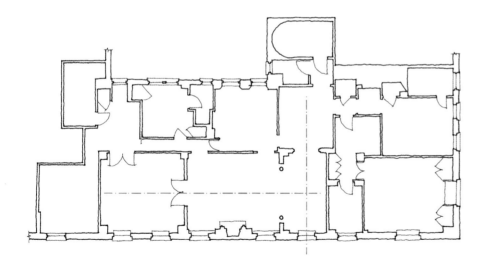

OPPOSITE The triumphal arch between the foyer and first reception room in the apartment reinforces the idea of passing from a semi-outdoor public space into a private indoor residence.

The foyer leads into the first reception room, from where the view to the right, set off by twin columns, looks through the drawing room toward the dining room where, on the end wall, is the climax of the enfilade—a glimpse of an exquisite watercolor mural.

To understand this apartment is to be aware of two levels of interpretation. The space may be viewed as a romantic Venetian pastiche, but also as a minimalist environment. Together these parallel realities give the apartment its feeling of nostalgia for the past as well as its sense of future.

OPPOSITE From the central drawing room in the "Venetian" apartment, the view in one direction looks toward the first reception room, and in the other toward the dining room. ABOVE The dining-room mural by Jean Charles Dicharry was inspired by a Pompeiian fresco (*see page 66*). The walls and ceiling around it are clay-colored so that they do not look too fresh or new in comparison with the mural. Visitors sometimes comment that the mural seems to be fading from the ground up. This appearance is not accidental. When it was first finished, the mural seemed too perfect to me, and the artist watched in horror as I took a rag with paint remover and started ruining some of his work. The resulting smudges suggest that rising damp, such as would have existed in an ancient Venetian palazzo, destroyed the paint, and the effect lends the room a feeling of elegant decay.

That attack is typical of my work. I set up a discipline; but if I think that it is becoming too refined, I deliberately violate it in order to let the occupants dominate the space.

A house that I designed in Arizona has two main axes that cross each other, and a third which is parallel to the first. One axis runs through four rooms, from the fireplace of the library at one end to the dining room, where the finale is the light that pours through a double-domed oculus in the roof on to the table (*see page 84*). The other leads from a two-story-high window, which frames the spectacular view of a mountain peak, to a channel of water that ultimately pours into a lap pool (*see following pages*), which itself forms the major part of the third axis.

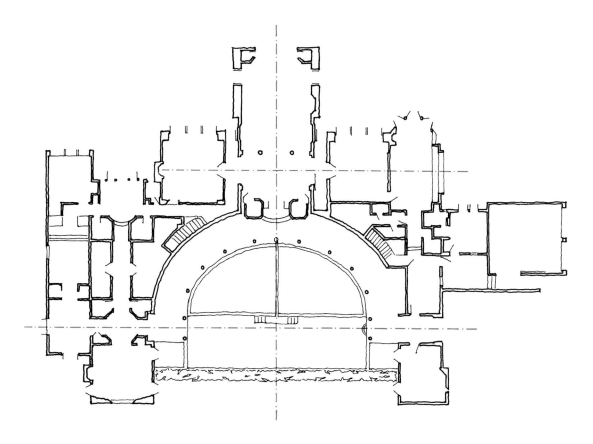

ABOVE My drawing of the ground floor of the Arizona house shows the three main axes in red.
LEFT The view from a small sitting room along the lap-pool axis is framed by a pair of columns that support the curving colonnade. The pair of semicircular marble seats on the edges of the pool double as diving platforms.

In the Arizona house, the axis from the framed view of a mountain peak to a thin channel and an expansive view of the desert (*right*) crosses the axis formed by the lap pool (*below*).

The idea behind the architecture of the Arizona house was to marry two seemingly unrelated ancient cultures. On to my memories of Rome's Villa Giulia (built by Vignola in 1553 as a country house for Pope Julius III), where a columned classical façade curves around a semicircular forecourt, I grafted the similar geometry of the remnants of New Mexico's ninth-century Pueblo Bonito, and added walls of Anasazi Indian stonework. The columns themselves are a marriage of ancient Rome and the traditional Southwest. They appear to be Doric but are actually replicas of a cactus that was growing on the property. The columns were carved in stone in Mexico, following a full-scale drawing of mine.

The lap pool came out of early conversations with the clients. They agreed that, in that desert context, the greatest luxury was water, so I made this theatrical water-feature the focal point of the plan.

Axial organization is a fundamental concept on which to build a design, and a relatively simple, easy way to arrange visual ideas. It directs attention to a sequence of objects and moves the eye through space. Just as the rhythms of music move through time, design rhythms move through space along the path you have predetermined. When used effectively, axis functions as the aesthetic Pied Piper, and never more so than in a garden.

Some of the greatest twentieth-century gardens illustrate this point. Among the most famous are two in England—Hidcote Manor, in Gloucestershire, designed by Major Lawrence Johnston, and Sissinghurst,

designed by Harold Nicolson and his wife Vita Sackville-West. Johnston was an American who moved to England because the climate was so much more conducive to gardening. He created the garden at Hidcote as a series of exterior rooms, to be experienced one after the other, just like walking through a great house, following major axes. The walls are tall hedges—of clipped yew, of pleached hornbeam on stilts, or of a tapestry of beeches; and the doors are narrow gaps giving only partial views of the next garden beyond. The long formal vistas entice the visitor to keep venturing onward with the promise of more treats to come.

LEFT At the far end of the red borders at Hidcote are two little pavilions; they sit at the crossing of two major axes in the garden. Here they act as sentinels at the entrance to the Stilt Garden, so called because of the avenue of pleached hornbeams that leads to an elegant gateway overlooking the countryside beyond; the cross axis, at right angles to this one, has a view that looks through the glazed French doors of the pavilions.

LEFT In the garden at Penns in the Rocks, in Sussex, created in the eighteenth century, an urn designed by William Kent beckons us on through the beech arch and along a close-mown path through a flowery meadow.

I used the concept of axis to solve a difficult problem posed by the wishes of clients for the garden of their Colorado home. Their house overlooks a lake and the land falls abruptly away from the house, dropping about 20 feet to the shore of the lake. The challenge was to fulfill the clients' request for a succession of gardens—from a Japanese to a Mediterranean to an English and finally to a shade garden—to be accommodated within this short distance. The solution was a tumbling brook that guides the visitor from one cultural happening to the next before it empties into the lake. The moving water that spills and splashes through the sequence of different gardens is the link that connects the gardens to each other and the house to the lake.

My garden at Robin Hill is actually a series of gardens: the Round Garden, the Gray Garden, the Allée, the Appian Way, and the Azalea Field. Rather than as "garden rooms," I think of these gardens as acts in an opera or a play.

I planned my garden so that it would be experienced sequentially, drawing you from small spaces to larger ones and from shade into full sun. I achieved the same effect indoors by painting a little entrance hall a dark color, and the two-story drawing room beyond it a pale hue. In house and garden, as you move from dark to light, and from small to large, your senses are manipulated by the changes in color and space.

Just as classicism taught me that an axis in a house should have a visual reward at each end, so I believe that no garden vista should be without a focal point or conclusion. At Robin Hill, the largest outdoor space, the Allée, was created by replanting an eighteenth-century cow path. Rhododendrons, birches, mountain laurels (*Kalmia latifolia*), and Japanese dogwoods (*Cornus kousa*) were brought in and underplanted with ferns and other shade-loving plants. The avenue finishes with a small garden—another act in the play. The focal point here is a huge seventeenth-century Tuscan olive jar made of terra-cotta. Behind the jar, to terminate the view, I planted three cone-shaped yew trees, clipped to simulate cypress. The trees are positioned in graduated scale to create the illusion that the Allée is longer than it is in reality.

When planning a garden, I often think of it as a hand, moving from the house in the palm to the fingers that reach out to the edges of the property. At the end of the fingers, the appropriate terminations could be a beautiful tree or shrub against a wall or hedge, an urn on a pedestal, or planting so luxurious that you might believe that you were entering a forest. In addition to the jar, other focal points at the end of the fingers in my garden include a sixteenth-century English horse-trough that ends the Appian Way, and a weathered millstone that terminates the orchard.

Most gardens also need secondary axes, running either at right angles to, or diagonally across, the main vistas, in order to create necessary links. At Robin Hill some of the secondary axes are walkable; others are purely visual.

Axis plays a key part in structuring the grounds at Robin Hill—several paths lead out from the house toward focal points. I took a cue from the architecture of the house and laid out the gardens in a long pattern that parallels the house. Plantings closest to the house are the most controlled but toward the boundaries of the property, they become wilder and wilder until finally they seem natural and unplanned.

The map shown here is both two-dimensional and three-dimensional. The aerial view of the garden is superimposed over the façades of the front and rear of the house. Sections of the building are also incorporated (see the elliptical staircase on the right side of the map), together with personal features such as urns and obelisks from the garden. This romanticized pastiche is the map of an imagined Arcadian landscape.

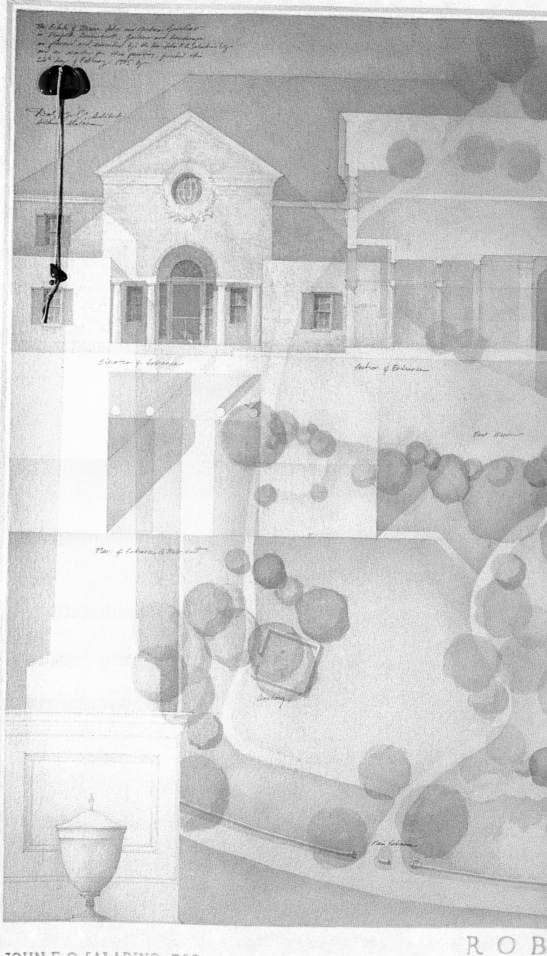

JOHN F. O. SALADINO, ESQ.

ROB
NO

IN HILL

FOLK
CONNECTICVT

CHAS. EVERETTE ARCHT

Yew trees clipped to form huge obelisks give depth and a sense of false perspective
at the end of a naturalized *allée* at Robin Hill. A terra-cotta olive jar is the theatrical
prize at the end of this living green corridor.

LEFT This vista, along a clematis-covered pergola, is one of the secondary, or cross, axes at Robin Hill. The main vista terminates in the bower of crab apple blossom seen in the distance on the right of the pergola.

LEFT AND BELOW One of the most romantic views at Robin Hill looks toward a bower created by training two crab-apple trees (*Malus sargentii*) over a rustic seat. In spring these are a cloud of white blossom, in summer a mass of small shiny red fruit, and in fall they make an arc of fiery red and tangerine leaves.

SCALE

From monumental to human

My former apartment in New York was named after this room—it was originally a ballroom. To control its vast size, I put in a 2-foot-high cornice, used overscale furniture including a 17-foot-long table, and created intimate niches with high-backed sofas.

ABOVE I urged my brother to take this photograph of a man standing in a doorway of one of the wings on the stage of the Teatro Olympico in Vicenza to illustrate the way in which the architect Palladio juxtaposed monumental, residential, and human scales.

ON THE SAME TRIP to Italy during which we first saw the Villa Rotonda, my brother and I went to see the splendid Teatro Olympico in Vicenza, designed by Palladio. It is an indoor amphitheater that houses one of the most beautiful stages and permanent sets in existence. The back section of the stage floor is canted upward, as are the wooden façades of the buildings that form the streets of the backdrop and which diminish in scale toward vanishing points. Patrons sit surrounded by a demi-lune arcade that Palladio built as a re-creation of the exterior of an open-air Roman amphitheater. The backdrop of the auditorium also has niches, columns, and statues painted in perspective. The effect is startling: although they are indoors, visitors are given the illusion that they sitting in an outdoor Roman ampihitheater. It was Palladio's handling of a multiplicity of architectural scales that made the greatest impression on me.

I became more keenly aware of subtle juxtapositions in structural heights when I worked among the ancient buildings of Rome a few years later. I came to realize that for both architects and interior designers, the importance of understanding and developing competence in using scale cannot be overemphasized. The most successful buildings demonstrate harmonious relationships in scale, whether externally to their surroundings, or internally to their occupants.

The lessons from Rome are seen clearly at work in my favorite Neoclassical room, the entrance hall of Syon House, near London. Remodeled in the early 1760s by Robert Adam, it is a re-creation of a Roman basilica—although the clerestory windows are glazed in glass rather than in alabaster as they would have been in ancient Rome.

Adam's work in this room is a textbook on using the three different scales that are integral to both architecture and interior design: monumental, residential, and human. The room is organized in horizontal layers using these three scales. Monumental scale is evident in the huge crown molding, or frieze, that encircles the room and appears to support the coffered ceiling. A third of the way down the walls from the ceiling is a lower, less imposing, cornice, which represents the residential scale and makes this vast room more easily assimilated. Finally, the smallest of the scales is used in the doorways, which relate to human proportions. Introducing this last scale enables the occupants to "move" through the three layers without feeling overwhelmed.

BELOW The entrance hall at Syon House, near London, designed in the mid-eighteenth century by Robert Adam, is a superb lesson in using three different scales to prevent a soaring space like this from overpowering the occupants.

41

Another fine example of a similar use of these three scales is William Kent's skillful scheme for Worcester Lodge at Badminton, in Gloucestershire. Kent made what could have been an overly vertical space (imagine being at the bottom of a milk carton) into a beautifully proportioned room by offsetting a huge frieze directly below the ceiling, adding a smaller-scaled cornice one-third of the way down from the ceiling, and giving the doors human dimensions.

I often look to the past, to Greek and Roman architecture and to the seventeenth- and eighteenth-century work of Inigo Jones and William Kent, for inspiration on reinterpreting and using the three scales. Above all, they show how good use of scale can prevent a vast space from being overpowering. When challenged with a huge room, I consciously use all three scales. My prime solution is to create "rooms within a room": in doing this, I often break up the floor area with carpets, and make use of folding screens and high-backed sofas. In creating more intimate spaces within a large room, there are three particular zones to address: the furnishings round the fireplace, those in a music or reading area, and those directed toward the view.

These techniques are demonstrated in my Connecticut drawing room. I manipulated the scale of the large space firstly by adding a huge crown molding, secondly by using folding screens that are 8 feet high, and thirdly by using sofas with 4-foot-high backs. Two sofas are close to the fireplace; opposite is a round draped table surrounded by chairs making a group that, in effect, speaks to the view, but also acts as a reading zone since I have bookcases on either side; lastly the piano creates a music area.

Insensitivity to scale is, in my opinion, what is wrong with much contemporary architecture and design. What are called "living" rooms are really more like lobbies with 14-foot-long sofas and coffee tables that have to be delivered by cranes. Understandably, people march right by them. Any sofa more than 8 feet in length prevents people from feeling at ease. The breakfast table is often where most of us like to linger longest; this is because the scale is human and therefore comfortable. If there is more than 7 feet between you and another person, you need a megaphone to converse.

Behind the high-backed sofa that makes a cozy cocoon within the large drawing room at Robin Hill is the baby grand piano, which makes another vignette or room-within-a-room.

The wall niches, with paintings by David Braly, were made to balance the large windows on the other side of the room.

Similar concepts are evident in my former New York apartment in a 1927 Romanesque-style building, once part of a five-floor penthouse belonging to the family of financier Jay Gould. During the 1930s the building was divided up and my apartment included the ballroom, a three-story-high room so enormous that it was nearly a double cube. It was a place where I could be experimental in a way that working for clients often does not allow.

To make this space feel inviting was a daunting task. The solution was to create a series of vignettes, and to use furnishings that were overscaled but appeared normal. (The chairs were so exaggerated in their size and angle of their backs that when I found them at Didier Aaron in Paris, I was convinced they must have been theatrical props whose back legs were made shorter to appear upright on the steeply raked stages of the period.) One vignette consisted of a 17-foot-long walnut Italian refectory table placed beneath a contemporary painting (*see page 38*). The size of the painting addressed the room and made the intimidating scale of the blank wall seem smaller. Intimate seating groups made other vignettes: these included the use of a folding screen behind a high-backed central sofa to create an "inglenook" where two people could comfortably converse. Another zone in the room was the music corner featuring a concert grand piano. All these outsize elements looked perfectly at home in the colossal space.

In my former New York apartment I manipulated the scale of my drawing room, once a ballroom 23 feet wide by 35 feet long and with a 23-foot-high ceiling, by visually dividing it into separate areas, for conversing, reading, and playing the piano.

By using three different
scales, the drawing room
of a house in California
no longer seems
intimidatingly large. A
huge 16-foot steel-and-
glass door immediately
tames, yet does not detract
from, the monumental
scale; the 7-foot-high
French doors on the
right reduce the scale
to residential; and a pair
of sofas, with a folding
tooled Spanish leather
screen behind one,
injects human scale.

My design for the drawing room of Las Tejas, a house in Santa Barbara, California, incorporates much that I learned from Adam's reworking of Syon House. The scale of the house links it to an opulent past—it was originally inspired by the sixteenth-century Villa Farnese near Rome, built by the architect Giacomo da Vignola for Cardinal Farnese, the grandson of Pope Paul III. In remodeling it, I wanted to maintain a respect for classical architecture and yet I did not want to create a mausoleum. I felt as though I was walking a tightrope.

I controlled the potentially overwhelming size of the drawing room with the scale of the *trompe l'oeil* coffering on the ceiling, and with the spectacular de Medici tapestry hung at great height. Flanking the tapestry is a pair of wooden columns which represent the residential scale, and human scale is seen in the pair of high-backed sofas of which I am so fond.

The way that the floor is divided, or zoned, by using carpets to identify specific areas also helps to break down the large size of the room. The center is given to two separate seating areas. One end of the living room is devoted to music with a grand piano, and the other is a study-library. There the wall is made up of bookcases; these surround a central, pedimented doorway set into a triumphal arch, which takes up the classical theme seen in the coffered ceiling and the Ionic capitals on the columns on either side of the tapestry.

Attention to scale keeps the great drawing room at Las Tejas, in California, from appearing cavernous. There is constant play among the three scales, from the large-scale coffered ceiling painted by Christian Granvelle, to the generously proportioned furniture.

LEFT The atrium at Las Tejas is at the heart of the house; it shows how scale has been handled to prevent this formidable space from being overpowering. The monumental scale of the room is tempered by the residential-scale size of the Tuscan columns of the arcade, while the fireplace niche pays homage to human scale.

The central section of the room has a retractable steel-and-glass roof. With the press of a button the whole ceiling slides open. When nights turn chilly, the ceiling is closed and people can retreat to the intimate niches under the arcades that run round the perimeters of the room. Here, cocooned in warmth from the radiant-heated floor, they can look out on to the cathedral-scale space and feel comfortable.

BELOW Effective use of scale can solve problematic spaces. In a little room at Las Tejas with a very high ceiling I paneled the room, keeping the paneling low to reduce the scale, and painted the upper part of the walls a shade of blue-gray. What had been an awkward space was transformed into a cozy refuge.

It is as important to have a variety of vertical scales outside the house as it is to have them inside. A flat garden is a boring one. If you have tall, mature trees, you are fortunate in that monumental scale will already have been established. If not, plant the largest you can afford. The middle scale can be represented by ornamental trees, large shrubs or manmade features such as a pergola or gazebo; and the smallest might include tall flowers, such as plume poppies or delphiniums, or decorative pots and urns.

The monumental-size Round Pond at Chatsworth, Derbyshire, which dates from the seventeenth century, is surrounded by residential-scale 'candle-flame' yews and beech hedges. As you walk round it, you come face to face with the eighteenth-century 'herms'—busts on pedestals, designed originally by Kent for Chiswick House—that people the hedge.

The garden at Chatsworth, in Derbyshire, is one of the grandest in England, yet it is never overpowering because at every turn elements bring the monumental scale down to a human one. The large Round Pond, for instance, is surrounded by tall clipped beech hedges, but inset into these are human-sized sculptures.

The Round Garden at Robin Hill also uses three scales. Around the stone perimeter wall is a huge circle of monumental 80-year-old red cedar trees. When we bought the property the area inside the wall was little but a muddy puddle, and so densely shaded that only fungus would grow. We dynamited a central section in order to construct a large circular pool—the second, middle scale. The third, human-scale, feature is the bower in a three-sided bay that interrupts the circumference wall. I floored it with stone and trained a rhododendron over it as a roof. The result is one of the loveliest spots in the whole garden; it is like a cozy inglenook in a great hall, a place in which to hide and look out on the almost public scale of the pool.

The Round Garden at Robin Hill is enclosed by huge cedar trees that tower over the waist-high stone wall. Inside is the middle-scale, 13-foot-diameter pool that I excavated, its lining painted the color of the surroundings to mimic nature. Finished with 12-inch coping, it has a carved white marble lotus fountain—my response to a Mogul garden—in the center. At the far side is the bower: with room for just two chairs, an iron settee and a small table with an Indian octagonal marble top, it is an intimate place to retreat to on a hot sunny day.

ILLUSION

Challenging the expected

The entrance to a New York apartment makes people gasp: the eggplant-colored walls are covered in rich fabric, the paintwork of the archway has been oxydized to look like bronze, that of the base board to resemble marble, while the elevator shaft is disguised as the base of a colossal column—the fluting is *trompe l'oeil*, the molding is real.

I WAS A YOUNG MAN in Rome when I fell in love with the idea of theatrical statements. I was on my way to the top of the Capitoline Hill to view Michelangelo's stately Piazza del Campidoglio—visitors ascend ramped stairs that serve to heighten their emotions in anticipation of arriving at the plaza with its central heroic-scale equestrian figure of Marcus Aurelius—and glimpsed through the Senate House on my right, the startling sight of fragments of the colossal statue of Constantine in the inner courtyard. The hand alone is as tall as a human being. This Alice-in-Wonderland-type of experience, perfectly timed, made me see things in a new way.

I remember the anticipation I experienced before visiting Chiswick House for the first time years later, by which time I was a lover of all things designed by William Kent. I already knew of its interiors by Kent, and that it was not a grand English country seat. However I had absolutely no idea that the rooms would be so charmingly intimate. Seeing them was a special moment of recognizing that rare combination of a "big/little" house. The "bigness" of this little house is summed up in Kent's treatment of an ordinary-sized corridor. With vision and artistry, he exaggerated the crown molding and the woodwork of the door-surround, divided the walls into panels, and crowned the door with a bust held aloft on an elaborate corbel, giving the passage great splendor. Visitors are distracted from the narrowness of the space and participate in a theatrical show as exciting as coming upon the Constantine fragments in Rome.

Kent's vision reinforced my feeling that no matter how small or modest they are, all homes should have some sense of drama—a little pageantry, to provoke delight and surprise. I don't know why so many people are afraid of the idea of theatricality. Perhaps because most of us have been raised on a diet of guilt that says if something does not keep us warm or we cannot eat it, it is a willful extravagance. For me, a house is much more than a mere shelter, it should lift us emotionally and spiritually.

OPPOSITE An indication of the size of the fourth-century fragments of the statue of Constantine is given by the 8-foot-high door of the courtyard in which they are stored at the Senate House on the Capitoline Hill in Rome. BELOW In Kent's hands what would have been a mundane corridor in Chiswick House, near London, erupts into a spectacular passage.

LEFT AND RIGHT Learning from Kent's example at Chiswick to challenge the expected and to make a functional space a source of everyday delight, I made the dressing room in an apartment in New York far more theatrical than the bedroom it serves. The entry is a nod toward a triumphal archway: the arch is made of an eighteenth-century American fanlight supported by slim columns. The end wall is mirrored, as are the doors of the floor-to-ceiling closets, and the woodwork has been sprayed with silver car paint, so that the room is a shimmering reflection of the light that pours into the bedroom from the window over the East River. To add to the theatrical feel, the ceiling of the bedroom is lacquered so that it, in turn, reflects the archway of the dressing room upside-down in its high-gloss finish.

BELOW LEFT The hallway that my late wife and I added on to our first house, an eighteenth-century forge, is in keeping with the style and material of the original building.

BELOW RIGHT This stairway continues the dramatically classical theme seen in the entrance on pages 54-5. The first step is made from one large block of silver travertine stone.

Entrance halls or foyers are highly significant to me. Far more than simply somewhere to wipe your feet or hang your coat, an entrance to any home is essentially a ceremonial space, a place to make the adjustment from the outside world, to close one door before opening the next, so I feel it should be clear and uncluttered; it is also a place that can be used to heighten anticipation, or whet the appetite for what is to follow. I cannot imagine a proper residence in which you are immediately thrust into the best room of the house. So when my late wife and I bought our first home in

Connecticut, and found that the house had no entrance hall, we created one by using an existing space and paneling it with old wood. Not only did that simple hallway allow visitors to stop, to make the transition from their journey, but it gave the illusion that the house was larger and more important than it was in reality. An entrance hall or corridor may be one of the very few places in the house where you can be truly daring. If clients express nervousness at dramatizing an entrance hall, I remind them that they—or their guests—are in there for about thirty seconds.

BELOW LEFT The most limited space can be made ceremonial: the entrance-hall end of this corridor has a vaulted ceiling papered in silver leaf, and the fan "windows" are mirrored to increase the sense of space.
BELOW RIGHT The oversize column and pestle and mortar beside the elegant stairs at Robin Hill is a surprise in both setting and scale.

The entrance hall of my former New York ballroom apartment exemplified my belief that rooms can deliver far more than mere need and practicality demand. Inspired by an ancient Etruscan tomb, it became a textbook for many of my design ideas. Nearly all the colors, textures, and shapes used in the entire apartment appeared in this area as a preview of what is to come.

From the elevator hallway visitors stepped into the oval foyer. The curved walls were plastered with the roughest of undercoats, because I believe that is the best covering for curved surfaces, while the straight surfaces were laminated in sheets of dull silvered metal. The shallow elliptical ceiling was lacquered a soft amethyst color to give the effect of a blurred upside-down reflecting pool. The way to the living room led through one of the metal walls. Here, so that old met new, I placed an intricately carved pine Adam doorway salvaged from a stately home in Norfolk, England. In the middle of the foyer, the epicenter of the apartment, was a 9-foot-tall steel beam encased in a Doric-style plaster skin. Down one side of the column was a 2-inch-wide opening purposely showing the steel inside the casing. The bleached oak parquet floor, which ran through every room, fanned out from the column like an open book.

Much of the effect of this foyer came from a series of contrasts in which each component exaggerated the other. The yin-yang of the room was rough with smooth, architectural and illusionary, retro and futuristic. The conjunction of these disparate elements created a theatrical event, and I hoped that the daring of the deed would make viewers see anew.

An Etruscan tomb (*above*) was the inspiration for the oval foyer in my New York ballroom apartment (*opposite*). The ancient tombs, known as mastabas, are reminiscent of igloos made of stone, each with a central column to hold up the roof.

OPPOSITE Thin glazing bars help to increase the illusion of the fragility of the glass, which is also emphasized by the thickness of the walls. This window of a house in Arizona was made to frame the spectacular view of the vertiginous mountain peak. BELOW A guest-room dressing table has been made into an "event," or theatrical set-piece, by the glove-leather skirt, by the antique oriental carpet hanging on the wall behind it, and by framing one mirror with another.

The juxtaposition of opposites is always effective; it is a theme that runs through all my work. I put ancient with modern, high gloss with matte, soft with hard: an antique mirror over a contemporary table, shimmering silk curtains with unbleached linen-covered walls, a velvet sofa against a rough brick wall.

Another consciously heightened contrast that I aim to achieve when designing a house is between the walls and the glazing. In pursuing the concept of the home as a sanctuary, I feel that a room should, if possible, have a feeling of substance and permanence in order to provide shelter from a world that threatens us with constant change and ephemerality. To exaggerate the solidity of the walls, the glass should look tissue-thin.

In my enjoyment of contrast, and of challenging the expected, I sometimes buy an ordinary beaten-up wooden flat full of herbs, perhaps of chives or flowering thyme. Instead of pulling the flat apart and planting the herbs in the garden, I clean the box slightly and place the herbs on the dining-room table with silver candle-sticks. Again, the juxtaposition of opposites, of rare and humble, jostles perceptions and, in this case, relaxes the mood of the dining room and the people in it. Growing an amaryllis in an old corroded pot and placing it on a highly polished console table, forcing country and city cousins to keep company, would have a similarly liberating effect and make each be seen with fresh eyes.

I aim to capture visual attention by challenging the predictable in many different ways. Taking objects out of context and presenting them in unexpected surroundings can cause people to stop mentally in their tracks. Placing a fragment of a garden statue in the entrance of my New York apartment startled visitors in the same way as the *torchère* in an East River apartment in New York. There I converted a grand-scale garden urn into an uplight, sitting it on a pedestal which actually concealed stereo speakers. Suddenly a dissonance was created. People's perceptions were subliminally reshuffled, causing them to wonder "Is this indoors or out?"

The use of wall paintings to bring the garden indoors has a long and distinguished history. In one of the houses in the ancient site of Pompeii in Italy, the walls are adorned with remarkable decorative frescoes depicting a

beautiful orchard of trees and flowers behind a low fence. Although unaware of the techniques of perspective, the artist pulls the viewer into the imaginary garden with a fence that bends in the middle of the room, and actual-size trees. This bewitching scene causes the occupants of the room to rethink their surroundings and wonder "What kind of space is this?"

The Pompeiian wall painting is an early example of an artist striving to break out of what I call "the tyranny of the box," the six planes composed of four walls, a ceiling and a floor, through visual illusion. It is a form of *trompe l'oeil* painting which was later developed and used to create imaginary space, to transform a mundane rectangular box into something spectacular, reaching a peak in the eighteenth and early nineteenth centuries in Europe. I am very fond of this kind of ambiguity.

LEFT Standing in the House of the Fruit Orchard (also known as the House of the Floral Cubicles), in Pompeii, one can imagine that its fourth-century occupants might have felt as though they were seated outside in a gloriously verdant garden.

LEFT Decorated in the early years of the nineteenth century, this enchanting room at Grovelands, near London, was painted to give the illusion of a birdcage set within a garden, with views of a romantic landscape beyond its confines.

When I designed the dining room at Las Tejas, I set out to challenge the accepted perceptions of indoors and outdoors. Las Tejas is a Mediterranean-style villa in Santa Barbara, California, constructed over forty years and involving three different architects. It was originally inspired by the sixteenth-century Villa Farnese near Rome, and I made references to these antecedents in the dining room. On either side of the French doors that open on to the garden are floor-to-ceiling *trompe l'oeil* frescoes evoking the illusion of dining in an Italian loggia with a view of an idealized landscape. Contributing to the illusion are immense Adam-style lead urns—outdoor ornaments never intended to be used indoors—on plinths that conceal stereo speakers.

BELOW LEFT This mural in a New York apartment was based on the Pompeiian fresco seen on page 66.

BELOW RIGHT This fresco by David Braly was inspired by the Villa Barbaro's *trompe l'oeil* architectural moldings. The chair, made of lacquered goatskin, stands for a pot out of which the Jurassic-scale acanthus is sprouting.

I love enigmas that force the viewer to rethink the boundaries of the real world. The profundity of the Impressionist painter Degas's observation that "To be a great artist you must be a tenacious liar" led me to turn my fascination with enigma into a principle in my own design work. I delight in the ways in which architecture mimics painting, and painting mimics architecture. I am drawn to things that are not what they seem and I pursue illusions that rearrange perceptions of reality. In art, unlike life, celebrating an untruth can have great merit.

I enjoy turning the commonplace upside down and shaking anticipated perceptions; it provokes people into seeing anew. But small rooms, especially those not much used like a dressing room or powder room, are the best ones in which to create the most fantastic effects, where one won't get bored by the shock— you wouldn't want a jack-in-the-box going off in your face all the time. A favorite trick of mine is to put the light switch in a dark powder room at an unexpected height; the impact of the surprise when the light is finally switched on is even greater because of the pause for the search.

BELOW LEFT The giant marble capital hollowed out as a sink challenges perceptions of scale, and the mirror stands proud of the wall, secure in the arms of the sconces.

BELOW RIGHT A centuries-old trick involving false perspective, a canted floor, and a half-column against a mirror causes the images to complete themselves in the mirror, creating the illusion of a long passage.

By exploiting the "gullibility" of the eye—its capacity to be deceived—you can make a modest room seem larger or more important. If you paint the entrance hall a rich, dark color and paint the living room beyond it a pale color, you will find that, as you pass from one to the other, your perception of the light-colored living room will make it seem larger by contrast with the dark entrance hall.

Other classic tricks include using the same color for all six planes—walls, floor and ceiling—of a room. This makes a seamless envelope, the dimensions of which are hard to perceive. It is also a good idea to use furniture that stands on legs so that you can see more of the floor area; and in low-ceilinged rooms it is best to keep all the furniture as low as possible—avoid high-backed sofas, for example. Hanging an overly large painting or tapestry will imply that the room is grander than it is. Of course, for this device to work successfully, some of the other furniture in the room must be underscaled, especially the lamps, which will destroy the illusion if they are not modest in scale. Creating a floor-to-ceiling window treatment also visually increases the size of a room. It increases the feeling of "air," and prevents the exterior view becoming shut off from the occupants' sight when they are seated.

In a Colorado lakeside house in the foothills of the Rocky Mountains I replaced the short doors and transoms in the somewhat narrow living room with 10-foot-tall windows and French doors that open directly on to the terrace. Now the living room has an unobstructed view of the garden and the lake and also appears larger. I also wrapped the glass round a corner so that the corner appears to dissolve, making the room seem larger still. I repeated the modular windows and doors so the view is framed like a multipaneled Japanese screen.

There is often scope for moments of great theater outdoors. When a client asked me to build an equestrian estate in Connecticut, I recalled Michelangelo's plan for the Piazza del Campidoglio in Rome. (This plan of three buildings, angled so that they create an outdoor room, also inspired Philip Johnson when he designed Lincoln Center in New York in the 1960s.) I built three barns to make a U-shaped piazza-like paddock, and replaced the statue of Marcus Aurelius with a horse trough in the center.

The outdoor arena allowed exaggeration on a grander scale than would have been possible in an indoor setting. The Roman-numeral clock face, which is 6 feet in diameter, is mounted on a square cupola over the one-story stable that is so grandiose that it allows the central low building to stand proud between its two tall neighbors; the two-story-high passage—recalling a Roman triumphal arch—with a view through to the landscape beyond was built so that a horse and rider could pass through it with ease; and the dovecote, seen through the arch (*below*) is actually three acres away and over 12 feet high.

Little is more dramatic in a garden than a performance arena, whether this is a theater or a stadium. The oval "green theater" at the Villa Imperiale at Marlia, near Lucca, has an auditorium and a raked stage with an arcaded backdrop and footlights in clipped yew. Dating from 1690, it remains a superb demonstration of the power of a "proscenium" to frame a view, and a lesson in how to manipulate sight lines in a garden.

BELOW The raised stage of the green theater at the Villa Imperiale at Marlia, near Lucca, is complete with footlights, a prompt box, wings, and an articulated backcloth. The figures are *commedia dell'arte* characters.

The magic of a ceremonial space made with living greenery inspired me to create an outdoor room at Las Tejas based on the idea of a Roman racetrack. When I saw the lozenge-shaped area, I felt that the original landscape architect must have seen the Piazza Navono or the Circus Maximus, both of which were used for chariot races. At Las Tejas, existing mature trees become the architecture of the circus while the spectators are represented by a pittosporum hedge. The columns at the end mark the royal box—conjuring up the possibility of Caesar appearing; and instead of horse-drawn chariots, there are beds of calla lilies racing around the track.

OPPOSITE The theatrical "racetrack" garden at Les Tejas is also a contained, secluded "room" that visually extends the indoor dining room from which it leads.

The concept of giving emphasis to a vista by framing it or using false perspective to create the illusion of greater space can overlap with axial planning. At Robin Hill I use birch trees like curtains in a theater, to frame the performance in the garden; they represent the draperies pulled back on a stage. The Allée becomes narrower as it recedes away from the house, and the impression that the space is much deeper than it is in reality is reinforced by planting larger trees at the start and smaller ones at the end. If it is feasible to make a path culminating in ascending stairs, this will further increase the sense of space.

The theatrical impact of one of the chief vistas at Hidcote is increased by monumental topiary birds on massive pedestals. Not only do they frame the view, but the sheer unexpected scale is dramatic in itself. In my garden there is a pair of huge peacock-like topiary birds that loom over the smaller plants at their feet. Large-scale topiary is inherently theatrical—in the tension between the forces of nature and the controlling hand of man—but when it is placed where it towers over its surroundings, its size and effect become more exaggerated.

You can create drama on an operatic scale in a garden. Sheer over-the-

RIGHT Looking toward the beech arch, the topiary birds perched on substantial plinths and silhouetted against the sky dominate the garden in the winter at Hidcote.

OPPOSITE A pair of topiary birds towers over the 'Queen of Night' tulips at Robin Hill. Everything in this part of the garden, which is predominantly gray in the summer, is planted in rows to reflect the vegetable garden that it used to be. The route here leads along the mown path and through the weeping cherry trees (seen beyond and to the left of the topiary) that act as curtains to the main garden performance.

top abundance is rapturous when you know that the effect is fleeting. The notion is similar to passing quickly through a dramatic entrance hall in a house. At Robin Hill 7,000 *Narcissus poeticus* bulbs herald the arrival of spring in the orchard. (I managed this by shamelessly asking friends to put in a few bulbs every time they came over.) It was this love of *coup de théâtre* that determined the seasonal planting of the Allée. In scenes that enfold one after the other, 2,000 white tulips in large diagonal drifts appear beneath the trees in the spring; in early summer these are replaced by masses of white foxgloves, which are followed by scented white 'Casablanca' lilies.

LIGHT

The Prime mover

The light from the window in the gable end of the roof of a house in Long Island throws mysterious shadows and enlivens the rafters. The window faces west, to make the most of the evening sun when the heat of the day is past. French windows at either end of the enfilade also exploit the slanting rays of morning and evening light.

THERE ARE CERTAIN PLACES to which I return again and again for inspiration. The Criptoporticus, the ancient underground galleries in Rome, and the Caldarium, the hot-water baths at Pompeii, are two such places. In both, the light that streams down through the openings in the roofs is jewel-like. Bathing in the Caldarium must have been an act that was more than a banal washing away of the soil of the day; it must have been a ceremonial, almost spiritual experience.

Sir John Soane's house in London, now a museum, is another source of continued inspiration. Soane understood how light energizes and brings

RIGHT The light wells in the the Caldarium excavated at Pompeii are positioned and angled so that they perfectly manipulate the quality of light in the interior. Like spotlights, they create an impact, and yet leave areas of shadow that are large enough to have allowed the bathers here some form of disceet privacy.

life to a room, and how it molds our experience of interior spaces, elevating architecture beyond being merely the means of keeping ourselves warm or cool or the rain off our heads. He revolutionized domestic architecture by the example of his own house, which he flooded with natural light. As well as putting immense windows in the building's façade, he made use of clerestory windows and skylights so that light pours in from above.

Thomas Jefferson demonstrated a similar understanding of the power of light when he introduced skylights to North America by installing sixteen in his home, Monticello, in Virginia.

LEFT Sir John Soane made full use of direct and diffused natural light in the breakfast room of his London townhouse. By placing convex mirrors into the groins of the baldachin ceiling, he deceives us into believing that the heavy wood and plaster canopy is a tissue-thin umbrella.

Thirty-five years after I first experienced it, the light in the Caldarium is still an influence on my work, and I continue to exploit the dramatic effects of overhead natural light whenever I can. For a house in East Hampton, Long Island, I designed an entrance hall with a 30-foot-high, steeply pitched ceiling. Taking inspiration from the local vernacular architecture, I left the ridge beams exposed. The space, like a cathedral transept, is lit by a triangular window set in the gable end, as well as by French windows at ground level (*see page 81*). The Caldarium also inspired the circular window in the second-floor bathroom of that house (*see page 90*), and a rib-vaulted ceiling in a house in Arizona (*left*).

In my view, no space without natural light is worthy of human occupation. Yet, judging by the vast numbers of people who start each day in windowless kitchens and bathrooms, twentieth-century design evolved ignoring the emotional power of natural light. This sad fact reminds me that in ancient Rome if a senator proposed war, and the Senate voted in agreement, he became the first general. Similar justice would suggest that architects should serve time living in the buildings or rooms that they designed without light.

The ceiling in the dining room in a desert home in Arizona culminates in a skylight. I wanted people to feel natural light pouring over them like water into cupped hands. This light-filled room, its entrance framed by symmetrical columns and massive, leather-wrapped doorways, is the conclusion of a long enfilade. It acts like a beacon: people seem drawn to it like moths to a candle. The effect at night is equally dramatic: the ceiling is just proud of the walls, and concealed in the gap all round the perimeter of the room are light sources that wash the silk walls with a soft gleam.

This small house in Connecticut, which I remodeled for some neighbors, is a celebration of natural light. It was what I called an "I Love Lucy" ranch house—an unpreposessing 1960s house—tacked on to a brick building that had once been the potting shed of a major estate. I began by revealing the rafters of, and putting skylights into, the kitchen in the old brick building (*opposite, center*). I then peeled away the plasterboard ceiling of the 1960s living room (*main picture opposite*); this added drama, height, and the opportunity for more skylights. I also set a tiny window into a niche so that light fell onto the built-in desk (*opposite, below*). Later I added a glass sunroom (*below, right*), and a huge screened porch off the kitchen (*opposite, top*), making a U-shaped house round a grass courtyard (*below, left*).

If a house or apartment has a spectacular view of the constantly shifting play of light on the landscape that surrounds it, I feel that it would be criminal to shut it out with heavy curtains. In one house I exchanged the modest windows with floor-to-ceiling glass panels to make the most of the lakeside view (*see page 73*); in another, I framed the dramatic scene of a vertiginous mountain peak with a double-story window (*see page 65*).

This room, in Florida, has gloriously uninterrupted views of the ocean, and catches all the available sun from early morning until late evening. The challenge was to make the most of the light, while alleviating the too-modern proportions of the room itself. My solution was to veil the windows with iridescent, almost totally transparent, fabric. These drapes bring an element of gentle, constant movement to the room, distracting attention from the blandness of the windows. The screens of sandblasted glass give some protection from the "gaudy light of day" when reflections from the sea make the room even brighter. The highly lacquered ceiling looks wet; not only do the reflections break up its flat expanse, but it adds a psychological feeling of cool water and, at night, it seems to shimmer like a lake.

Unlike the mercurial quality of natural light, artificial light is static and can be controlled at will. An integral part of the design of a room, it can radically alter mood, and can highlight good features or disguise bad ones. If you think of light not as light sources, but rather as the complex orchestration of levels and kinds of light, you will become the conductor who controls the concert. It is crucial that lighting is considered from the inception of a project. All too often people invest months and a small fortune decorating a room and then, just prior to the great unveiling, they rush out and buy a few lamps, thus betraying all that has been spent.

This bathroom uses natural and artificial light in a dramatic and practical way. Light from the transom window, echoed in shape by the bath and recalling the Caldarium at Pompeii, is supplemented by light from French windows on either side of the room that catch morning and evening sun, and from (unseen) windows over the sinks. At night, uplights hidden above the cupboards, downlights over the sinks and table, and several lamps provide the light.

In the drawing room of our first house, decorated in 1970, ambient light came from tiny light sources in the bookcases and channels of low lighting on top of the beams. Mood light came from a classic Noguchi paper lantern, from a desk light and from the glass lamp that I designed, all of which were on dimmers so that they could be turned up to become work lights, and also from groups of candles.

When I am planning the artificial light for a room, I look at three zones: above head level, eye level, and below knee level; and at three different types of light: ambient, work, and art. Ambient light should anonymously illuminate an interior, and demarcate the shape and dimensions of a space. Work light, for reading and sewing, should be on dimmers so that when you do not need the very bright light you can transform the high levels of light into mood lighting. What I call art light is either to bathe paintings or other works of art with a specific kind of illumination, or to create accents and effects that are decorative in themselves—like an uplight hidden behind a plant that casts wonderful lacy shadows on the ceiling and walls. Art light can also be used to evoke a particular mood or atmosphere, such as candles on the dining-room table.

What I seek in the design of ambient lighting, the most difficult type to handle, is an elusive quality. It is at its best when it comes from several, subtly orchestrated sources, and it should never be confrontational or harsh. Do not give away all the sources if you can help it, but try and conceal them in coves and behind moldings.

For more general light, you can, if your taste is modern, rely on ceiling downlights and mask the bulbs with lenses. If you are a traditionalist, I would suggest using wall sconces with shades. For chandeliers in period rooms, my choice would be hand-blown Belgian bulbs with candle-size sockets rather than the standard Eddison base; and in addition, I would either keep the dimmer very low or use small shades.

I used light to evoke an emotional response in my ballroom apartment. The foyer had no natural light, and I deliberately kept the artificial lighting levels low so that it was a shock to step into the enormous drawing room so flooded with light that you might almost be outdoors. North and south light poured in to the room through three vast windows with sills set well

Concealed sources in the cornice of the vestibule in my ballroom apartment washed the ceiling with light, drawing attention to its vaulted shape. The decorative painting was a playful allusion to family history: my late wife, whose astrological sign was Pisces, was represented as a dolphin being ridden by my son in the guise of a putto. To right and left are my and my son's signs.

above head height. In order not to block the light, I covered these with gossamer shades, made from fabric fittingly called "opalin crista," or "dragon-fly's wing." At night their iridescence gently reflected the room's artificial lighting. French doors brought in more light, seeming to hint at a garden beyond, though in fact they opened on to small balconies far above the busy street below.

Artificial lights were concealed in the window sills so that the windows continued to appear as though they were the chief light sources after dark. Additional light emanated from the niches that contained sconces on either side of the French windows, again imitating the direction of the natural light. These niches were lined with brushed stainless-steel panels to reflect the light in a diffuse glow.

LEFT The drawing room in my ballroom apartmet was flooded with natural light during the day; and because most of the ambient light sources were hidden in the window sills, artificial light seemed also to emanate from there. The walls in the drawing room typified my affinity for modern ruins. The feeling of age and decay was achieved by mixing instant coffee with the plaster, and then turning on the radiators full blast so that parts of the walls dried faster than others, resulting in a patina in which the color varied from dark taupe to pale bone. In some areas the finish crackled like a Chinese glaze.

ABOVE LEFT AND RIGHT Sandblasted glass doors that can be rolled aside, patterned in trelliswork to echo the 1927 "Tudor" window, divided the dressing room and bathroom in the ballroom apartment to make a comfy niche. The cupboards on either side of the dressing-room window were covered in high-gloss laminate to reflect the light. The artificial ambient light sources, along with extractor fan and smoke alarm, were hidden above the floating ceiling, while stronger, work, light came from the downlights above the sink and from behind the panels of sandblasted glass that flank the sink.

Most people make the mistake of thinking that good lighting has to do with quantity, but the brighter the bulb and the higher the wattage, the harsher, colder, and more blue the light. Instead of using a 75-watt bulb, a better alternative is to use three 25-watt bulbs. They provide a softer, warmer cast as the lower wattage is closer to the red end of the spectrum.

When you are planning work light, you must decide whether or not you want to draw attention to the lamps. I happen to be a non-lamp person, so I use the simplest that I can either design or find. In the realm of lighting classics, I would cite Noguchi paper lanterns for the quality of light they give. I also love the thin tubular lamps that Cedric Hartman designed, now in the permanent collection of the Museum of Modern Art, New York. The Morsa lamp, another favorite, is utterly simple and gives a soft glow through a rice-paper shade. And the shade is pre-wrinkled, so you do not have to worry about children knocking over the lamps. I would like to think of my own lamp as a classic: it is simply a clear glass cylinder with a shade—as close as I can come to a non-lamp. The underside of the shade has a saucer shield of translucent white Plexiglas, so that when you are seated you do not get a harsh glare in your eyes. I am also very fond of using silver-bottom bulbs to avoid suffering the glare of a naked bulb.

For traditionalists, I recommend antique tole lamps. They are conservative in scale and can be placed anywhere without distracting from a period-style interior. The simplest candlestick lamps in ceramic or wood are also

I designed the Tripod lamp, which is still in production, in 1984 specifically to take three 25-watt bulbs instead of the usual single 60- or 70-watt bulb.

appropriate. I think that candle bulbs with exposed filaments turned all the way up look very rude, so unless you are willing to dim the light bulbs way down to just a glimmer, I suggest using little shades. I still use the shades I started making thirty years ago out of brown paper bags—they give a wonderful, tallow-like glow that is normally only produced from mica, which is very hard to come by now.

The color of all lampshades is very important. I generally prefer translucent white or ivory shades, especially onion-skin paper shades and beige craft-paper shades, rather than opaque ones for the more diffuse effect they give and the gentler light. Opaque shades are best when they are the color of the lamp base.

Lights turned up to their brightest at night look vulgar to me, because there is no natural light outside for balance. An overcast afternoon is the time that artificial light needs to be brightest.

When I design art lighting I try to imitate nature. Imagine a full moonlit night in a park, the soft illumination of the trees, the dark ground around a glistening pond. The light is ethereal and seems to emanate from the shimmering water. How is it possible to emulate that? If you have a highly waxed floor and a plant in a beautiful terra-cotta pot or marble urn or copper bucket, a concealed light behind the plant will produce leaf patterns in the blurred reflection of the waxed floor at night. These patterns, the lacy effect of shadows playing across the floors and walls, will begin to duplicate what happens on a moonlit night when the trees are in full leaf.

I designed this non-lamp in 1970 and it has been in production ever since. Known as the Saladino lamp, it is so unobtrusive that it seems to fit into almost every type of interior, whether period or minimalist.

At Robin Hill, tall candles on the table are mixed with vases of single flowers whose heads are at the same height as the candle flames, which are above eye level.

On the sideboard, which I designed of matte black cold-rolled steel, is a pair of Italian candlesticks. Their shades have mirrored linings which increase the light that the candles give, and also add their own sparkle.

Candles, whether votive or tapers, make an evening more romantic and ceremonial. Candles do not have to be at eye level. Votive candles look wonderful placed on silver trays on low tables. I have a client who had a fireplace with a flue that had been sealed and she put several votive candles of different sizes in the fireplace.

I like three kinds of light on the dining table. I often put votive candles on the table, usually one in front of each place setting. These make the silver and crystal, as well as any silver or gold on the china, sparkle. I also use several very exaggerated candlesticks with the tallest candles I can find—15 to 24 inches high—in the middle of the table. The candles are very theatrical and the source of the flame, which can be irritating when it is at eye level, is above head level. (If you prefer lower candles, my advice is to use tiny shades.) In addition, I use ceiling downlights, at a very low point on the dimmer, to give the whole table top a soft even glow. If you have a chandelier, I would suggest converting it from electrical use so that it holds real candles.

As for candle colors, I normally like only shades of white and neutral. However, for very formal evenings, I use black candles in silver sticks. There are times when I suppose you could use colored candles, although I have never found out when—even at Christmas they always look to me like crayons gone mad!

Kitchens, bathrooms and bedrooms need special kinds of lighting. For kitchens I tell people to keep the ceiling lighting in check and put more light under the wall cabinets. You need light on the work surface, not on your head! A kitchen with massive amounts of ceiling light casts shadows on the very counter where you are working.

In a bathroom I think that you should be surrounded with light. I often set the sink in a niche, push a downlight in the top recess and make the flanking walls sandblasted panels of glass backed by thin sheets of white glass with incandescent frosted bulbs behind them.

In a bedroom I often use swing-arm wall lights, or sometimes table lamps on either side of the bed instead. And I suggest that those little lights that clamp on to the pages of a book are a very civilized and thoughtful idea for insomniacs who do not wish to disturb their partner.

LEFT The walls of the this sink alcove are mirrored so that all the lights are reflected, and therefore doubled in intensity. The vanity is a sheet of glass so that the stainless-steel sink appears to be free-floating; and the Queen Anne mirror becomes a romantic icon in the minimalist setting.

RIGHT The chief source of light in the bedroom of the ballroom apartment was the huge window. During the day, privacy was maintained by a thin mesh, electric solar-screen shade. Its place was taken after dark by an amethyst-colored, unlined silk blind. Hidden in the window soffit were artificial downlights so that even at night, the window was aglow. Two lamps on the sofa table behind the bedhead served as reading lights.

The lighting in the dining room of a client's Santa Barbara home shows how interesting effects are created when light and dark play against the architecture of a room. I used down-lights in the ceiling, small lamps on the sideboard, tall floor candelabra, a candle chandelier, and concealed uplights in the plinths of two of the floor candelabra.

Light is even more obviously the prime mover outdoors than in: without it, nothing will grow. But although the dramatic effects of light—natural as well as artificial—are more difficult to manipulate in the garden than in interiors, the results can be even more satisfying.

Natural light is always changing. The daily cycle echoes the seasonal one: as the sun or summer heats up, bright golden sunlight becomes almost white-hot before cooling to the glow of early evening or fall, and then to the blue light of late evening or winter. There are also days when clouds turn the light from glaring to gray. If you exploit these light conditions, the garden can become far more dramatic and the sun will become your ally in stimulating the viewer's emotions. An interesting garden structure, for example, will show up best in the low slanting sun at the beginning or end of the day, and, placed carefully, will cast elegant shadows.

Shade and sunshine provide natural chiaroscuro. Even a path through an orchard looks brighter in contrast to the shadows cast by the living umbrella of the trees. It is this kind of tonal contrast, between darkness and light, that I like to echo in the planting of a garden. Even the smallest areas offer opportunities to create vivid vignettes. Shady areas can be lightened by using plants with bright or limey-green foliage, or with flowers of white or blue—the two colours that show particularly well in low light. In a sunny

Beneath the large maple trees off the motor court at Robin Hill, I planted vivid green ferns, euonymous, and periwinkle to brighten the shade, adding white narcissi for spring; I left the walls a dappled white to add more light. A climbing hydrangea, which is also good for shady walls and produces large but not too dense heads of white flowers in late summer, makes an arch over one of the guest-room windows.

area, dark evergreen hedges make especially effective backdrops for pale schemes. Silver-leafed trees and shrubs, such as a weeping pear, Russian olive, artemisia or lavender, as well as tall white flowers, such as delphiniums, show up superbly against yew, especially if the hedge is clipped so that the contrast of form between the static, flat plane of the yew and the rustling foliage or swaying fronds in front is also apparent. The drama is heightened in strong sunlight when the tonal differences are further increased.

I think one of the most overlooked aspects of gardens is their effect at night. Perhaps no one understood this better than Vita Sackville-West when she made the White Garden at Sissinghurst. Sadly, few people are able to see it when it is at its most magical, glimmering in the moonlight. But because Sissinghurst consists of several buildings, the family had to cross the garden

every evening on their way to their bedrooms, so she would have experienced the luminosity of the white flowers as darkness fell.

If you use your garden at night, you will know that not only do plants release their scent after sundown, but that white shows up better then and for longer than any other color. That is one of the reasons I have planted the Allée with so many white flowers: at night it looks like a stage set for a ballet. Paradoxical as it might seem, the eye can make out blues well after reds or oranges have receded into near-black, because our blue receptors continue to work better in dim lighting.

To make the most of warm summer evenings outside, I recommend assisting natural light with artificial light. However, with the exception of specific lanterns in areas where you wish to sit, the light sources should

OPPOSITE The White Garden at Sissinghurst in the misty light of fall looks almost as mysterious as it does in the summer twilight. Most of the flowering plants are over, but a few white antirrhinums and marguerites are joined by the blooms of the potato vine; the billowing clouds of ghost-pale artemisia are backed by a spirea and echoed by lower-growing, small-leaved helichrysum and woolly-leaved stachys.

LEFT The tonal contrast between the dark ever-greens—prostrate mugo pine and clipped yews—and the pale trunks of silver birches and the whitewashed wall at Robin Hill remains constant through the year. Even in bad weather the white elements lift and lighten this area on the bluestone gravel terrace close to the house.

always be concealed. I hide amber lights among the underplanting at the base of birch trees; this highlights the beauty of their silvery bark. A down-facing light hung high in an important tree will create a beautiful pattern of branches over the lawn, while discreetly placed floodlights can enhance the moonlight, silhouetting the leafy branches of towering trees.

It is always worth considering lighting the main axis in your garden. But instead of putting ugly commercial lights every few feet along the path, a light-colored path, constructed perhaps of tiny gray or beige gravel, would be bright enough to reflect light fixed in a few selected trees. If you place an exquisite lantern at the end of the vista, visitors will find themselves drawn, like fireflies, to this beautiful focus.

LEFT AND OPPOSITE These two photographs were taken in the outdoor dining area of a client's house in Santa Barbara, California, as the sun went down one summer evening. As well as all the candles on the table, I concealed tiny lights in the crossbeam of the pergola to boost natural light, and hung cool blue downlights in the trees to simulate moonlight.

Remember that light from the house will inevitably be cast into the garden. A fluorescent-lit kitchen can destroy the fragile mood outdoors at the flip of a switch, so modify its harsh effect either by using shutters or by fixing a concealing baffle on to the light fitting. Even the incandescent light that spills out from a drawing room needs to be balanced by low-wattage lights concealed among the plants. If you have a sitting or dining area, you should, for safety's sake, throw light on any changes of floor level, and on the pathway that takes you there, but never spoil the atmosphere of a night garden by overilluminating it. Just as it is true for interior lighting, so it is for the garden: it is the *quality* of the light that matters not the quantity—here too less is often best.

COLOR

Metamorphosis and harmony

The dining room at Robin Hill is a symphony of shimmering, cool colors in the summer. The glossy celadon woodwork, antique white Marseilles tablecloth and blue-white chintz slipcovers, and especially the gossamer-fine spun-fiberglass roman blinds, mounted in eighteenth-century style, gently reflect the color of the pale amethyst walls. In winter the slipcovers are removed to reveal the light taupe wool upholstery, bringing seasonal warmth to the room.

WHEN I FIRST ventured into the dome area of the townhouse that belonged to Sir John Soane, the last great Georgian architect of England, I was overcome by what I saw: it is a catacomb, over two stories, of excessive collecting. His plunder from the ancient Mediterranean world—statues, busts and urns, fragments of columns, sections of friezes, finials, and plaques, capitals and corbels of every size and shape—is calculatingly hung from the walls, or pieces are stacked on top of each other like so many totem poles. Lit by a large domed skylight, the colors of the stone and marble vary every hour of the day, and with every flicker in the weather. The cumulative effect is of an abstract interior, an envelope enclosing endless variations of

RIGHT The dome area of Sir John Soane's house in London is almost exactly as he left it when he bequeathed it to the British nation as a museum in 1833. His collection of Greek, Roman, and Egyptian antiquities is arranged not by periods or culture, but as a sumptuous collage, and the first impression it gives is of a kaleidoscope of shades and tones of cream, clay, taupe, and gray.

one overall, elusive color. It reminded me of the scheme John Fowler used when he was asked to restore the entrance hall at Syon House in the 1960s (*see page 41*). These subtle nuances of color make a deeply satisfying harmony.

Although the central hall of mirrors in the Amalienburg outside Munich is so different in every respect from the Soane house, the essence of its appeal to me is in the cumulative, shimmering effect that cannot be pinned down to just one or two colors. This room, the epitome of eighteenth-century Rococo style, is elegant, mirrored, and layered in many tones of pale blue, cream, and silver leaf. The reflections and pale hues create an ethereal interior landscape that I longed to emulate as soon as I saw it.

LEFT The hall of mirrors in the Amalienburg, which was built in the 1730s in the grounds of Munich's Nymphenburg Palace, was designed to blur the boundaries between the ceiling and walls, and between the room and its surroundings. Ceiling-height glazed doors bring the outside into the room, which itself has a pale sky-blue ceiling. Exquisite silver-gilded stucco fronds and endless mirrored reflections make a timeless confection of blue, creams, and silver.

Color palettes that you have seen and liked are a good starting point, but need not be duplicated exactly. Use the overall effect of the original to create your own schemes. The Amalienburg was the inspiration for the color scheme in my dining room at Robin Hill. The walls are pale amethyst and the woodwork is finished in a high-gloss celadon. Bleached floors, shiny platinum-colored chintz tablecloth, and blue-white slipcovers create a cool oasis that is an echo of the icy sparkle of the German palace that inspired it.

The colors I like best are those that change constantly with the light, and that do not reveal themselves immediately. These are the colors that are sensual for me, as intimate as someone's touch. I have always been intrigued

with colors that make you wonder "Is that celadon or is that gray? Is that beige or is that taupe?" And I love the chameleon colors that vary with the time of day and, when seen under artificial light at night, become either richer and deeper, or seem to disappear completely. These are the colors that I call nuanced or metamorphic.

The most subtle nuanced colors should have a luminous quality, like the frescoed walls of Italian palaces where the color is mixed into the wet plaster. The best way to achieve this effect, if your budget permits, is to have the walls lacquered. A less expensive way is to have them coated with a thin layer of new plaster, and then, once they have been painted the color you

LEFT At Robin Hill I mixed the color of the shutters to match the slate roof, the lead flashing and Adam urns, and the gravel on the terraces. It is difficult color to define as it is simultaneously gray, green, and blue. Seen in the cool light of winter, the orchestration of tone is clearer than in the bright light of summer.

LEFT The walls of the drawing room at Robin Hill are an undefinable deep taupe color; it has a red base so that at night, when the room is lit by incandescent bulbs, it looks very warm, but daylight makes it looks cooler and more recessive.

The fireplace is by Grinling Gibbons; I hand-stripped the layers of paint, leaving it so that the details of the carving are its main attraction. The painting by Robert Cartwright that stands above the mantelpiece is itself a patchwork of nuanced colors.

want, finished with a coat of polyurethane. The latter technique is best reserved for deeper, warmer colors because the polyurethane will first darken the color and then, as it oxidizes in the light, will eventually turn yellowish.

We are often more objective and adventurous about color in our dress than in our homes because our clothes can so easily be taken off and changed. However, in a certain sense, it is possible and very useful to "try on" room colors. Spend a small amount of money, buy a few quarts of paint, and color a corner. Look at that area when you wake up in the morning, and in the evening when the lights are on in the room. Live with the color for a month before going ahead and painting the whole room. We commonly test a roll of wallpaper—why not do the same with paint?

Relying on paint chips is unsatisfactory. Color multiplies in intensity when the square footage increases. What appears an acceptable color on a small chip can become very aggressive when enlarged. It is often wiser not to leap to what seems, at first, like an obvious choice. Rather than settling immediately for the color that you *think* you want, my advice would be to select a color a few shades lighter; that way the color of the finished painted space will often have the effect that you thought you would get from the small sample.

The sitting room at Robin Hill is a winter room, so I used flat paint on the vaulted ceiling and walls. The color, however, is metamorphic: it changes with the light, from cinnabar-red to dusty rose, or brown. When I stripped the 1930s green paint off the antique American paneling, I left all existing traces of the original 1680s surface. At that time it would have been painted in faux-marble to resemble the costly chimney breasts of England.

Some colors should only be used in a limited quantity. Shocking fuchsia on a soft pillow can be wonderful, but I cannot imagine using it to cover a whole sofa. On the other hand, metamorphic pale pinks and amethysts, both of which flatter a variety of skin tones, can be used more widely. Although most people avoid amethyst when decorating—they think of it as lavender and run in the other direction, it is one of my favorite colors.

LEFT The intense fuchsia pillow makes a stunning color accent, but needs the balance in tone provided by the 1820s folding screen. The reveal behind the sofa is a pale echo of the scheme: it was painted fuchsia and then sponged with taupe.
ABOVE Bronze silk velvet and pale amethyst silk are muted enough to cover a sofa and chair.

When colors are repeated they can act like a unifying musical theme, linking the rooms of a house. Using a background of muted, related colors is one way of doing this, and works especially well in rooms that lead into each other. Repeating accent color is another way of linking spaces.

I am very fond of periwinkle blue and this color appears in drifts throughout the house at Robin Hill. As you pass from the dining room and enter the breakfast room (*right*) the blue is repeated on the slipcovers of the chairs. I have continued the theme in the garden with many blue flowers, including ground cover of *Vinca minor* 'General Bowles' (*above*).

The "Venetian" New York apartment, which consists of a series of rooms that open up into one another, is unified by a harmonious color palette—various shades of cream, clay, celadon, pale blue, gray, and oyster, leavened by touches of silver and burnished gold. These colors evoke the pellucid light and aqueous shadows of a misty day in Venice.

The rooms of the New York apartment seen here and overleaf are linked by a palette of rosé and clay colors, as well as by variations on the classical theme. The watered silk on the walls of the drawing room (*left*) is my response to the clients, who specifically asked me to give them a watermelon-pink backdrop for their superb collection of antiquities. By echoing the color on the ceiling, in the rough-textured roman blinds, and in the window woodwork, what might have been a somewhat anonymous space is made into a cocoon.

The proportions of the two windows have been repeated in the mirrored alcove on the right in order to give this end of the room symmetry and thus a strong axis. The focal point—the magnificent Roman torso—is further emphasized by being framed by two Doric columns. The clay color of the columns is taken along the crown molding, in which the egg-and-dart detail is picked out in tarnished gold leaf, and into the conservatory dining room (*above*) in the paintwork and tablecloths.

The magenta damask tablecloth in the small, more intimate dining room (*right and below*) of the apartment seen on the previous pages picks up the rosé theme. The crown molding of the drawing room is repeated here and its classical Greek motif is echoed in the acanthus-leaf corbel that supports the marble shelf beneath the painting. Taupe and beige striped silk curtains and fabric-covered walls make a visually and acoustically calm backdrop.

For a house in Arizona, where there is unrelenting sunlight and little water, I used muted colors that acted like balm to the searing heat. Except for the bedroom (*far right*) which, at the clients' request, mingles Anglo-Indian and Hispanic influences, the palette reflects the hues of the desert vegetation: teal, sage-green, gray, umber, beige, and cream. According to the owner, "When it's 110 degrees outside, it's a relief to walk in to these colors."

Color can be used to highlight or play down objects, and to manipulate space in subtle ways. Seen against a background of pale, almost monochrome tones, antiques or period-style furniture will be set off and highlighted like pieces of sculpture. To reinforce a sense of space, the major piece of furniture should be the same color as either the walls or the floor. For example, a white refrigerator will recede into a white room, but in a dark blue room will stand out like a bandaged toe on a bride.

The most important thing about color is that it cannot be isolated. Every color is only ever seen in juxtaposition with other ones. The importance of juxtaposition can be easily demonstrated if you are trying to choose a white. When you put eight of your favorite whites on a board so they all touch, the color you are looking for will become evident: one white will seem pink, another cream, and another gray-green.

Wherever color is used in the home, it is always a union, a marriage with the occupants of the room, or with the way a room faces, or with what is

outside. Colors used in interiors should complement what is visible outdoors. The audacity of a marigold-colored room works in the cold gray northern light of Ireland or Scotland, where there is relatively little bright sun; the brilliance of the color is tempered by the sobriety of the climate. But a room painted the same intense yellow in desert-like Texas would make inhabitants feel on fire indoors. For the same reason, white is generally not a good choice where there is glare outside: for example in Michigan, which is covered in snow for so much of the winter. Instead, I might choose peach or perhaps the green of spring. In contrast, California's veiled light allows the eye to enjoy many shades of white without the associated glare.

Color should be used in a way that is appropriate to the environment, so that it reinforces the architecture, balances the natural conditions, and nurtures the souls of the inhabitants of the house. In choosing colors, I often advise clients to follow nature's lead. One particular client loved the peachy gleam of the interior of a sea shell that she had. Her apartment, on a lower floor of a pre-World War II building in New York City, did not have wonderful views or much natural light, so the sea-shell color in high-gloss paint worked well in her slightly gloomy space. However, she then moved to an apartment on a high floor with a view of the water, where the peach color would not have been so successful. So we concocted a new color that was influenced by the view of the water and the client's collection of celadon ceramics.

ABOVE A French mantelpiece made from cipolin Italian marble includes the same quiet tones of celadon and taupe that were sponged on to the walls behind it.
RIGHT The screen is made from hand-blocked, early eighteenth-century wallpaper.

This apartment has such an affinity with the East River in New York City that looking out of the windows one feels as if the drawing room might be cantilevered over the river.

The ceiling has been painted in high gloss to make the most of the quality of natural light which, reminiscent of that in a Venetian palazzo, seems full of watery reflections. The colors of the river inspired those of the walls.

By breaking up the space, allowing for several intimate clusters of furniture for intimate conversation or simply gazing out of the window, the huge floor space is prevented from being overwhelming.

My predilection for natural, muted colors has not changed dramatically over three decades. The bedroom in Robin Hill (*left*) was decorated in the 1970s. I used a honey-colored leather screen as a headboard. The central section is fixed to the wall, leaving the two end panels to be hinged forward to emphasize the feeling of being cocooned in bed. The walls are faded blue-gray-green, and the woodwork and area below the dado are a deeper shade.

This bedroom in a Palm Beach house (*center*) was decorated in the 1980s. The honey-colored screen appears here in panama straw—the type used to make hats—and the folds are larger than my Connecticut one so it is better able to shield the glare of the stronger Florida sun.

This New York bathroom (*right*) was decorated in the 1990s. The honey color comes from sycamore wood, stained a deeper-than-natural shade to give warmth to the marble floor and fittings. The rosé-colored wingback chair in the dressing room, and the crown molding, links it to other rooms in the apartment (*see pages 126-9*).

BELOW The Purple Border at Sissinghurst at midsummer overflows with many of my favorite flower colors. The blues, purples, soft lilacs, and wine-dark reds are here leavened with silvery eryngium and the yellowing hips of *Rosa* 'Geranium'.

RIGHT The terraced area just outside the doors that lead to the dining room at Robin Hill is planted with flowers in blue and white, the colors that show up best in the evening light. I like to make direct links between the garden and house—for example, by planting pots of flowers that bring the wall color from the interior of the house outside.

The emotional power of color in the garden—to excite or calm—is brilliantly demonstrated at Sissinghurst, where the garden is designed as a series of enclosed spaces, each of which has its own predominant color theme. Most famous is the White Garden (see page 108), but, among others, there are also the Cottage Garden, which is planted entirely with fiery, sunset colors that demand attention and seem to give out heat, and the Purple Border, which is a magisterial mix of blues, purples, clarets, and magenta, and creates a brooding, reflective atmosphere.

The colors that I prefer to use in the garden are the cooler tones of blue, lavender, rose, and wine-red, set off with highlights—or rivers—of bright, sparkling white and lashings of silvery-gray foliage. I tend to shy away from warmer colors, especially any reds on the orange end of the spectrum.

The colors with a blue bias are the recessive, unassuming colors. They remind us of the sea and sky and far-distant mountains, and create tranquil, restful moods. Hot colors are bold and showy and conjure up an aura of excitement. They are known to raise blood pressure and heart rate and, like strong colors inside, I find them unsettling in large quantities. I do, however, have a planting of scented coral-colored rhododenrons in the wilder section of my garden. In the spring, when they seem to light up the clearing in the woods, their red-gold glow is particularly welcome (*see page 140*).

Color in a garden does not come just from flowers. I remember lying down in the grass when I was a child and being aware of the taupe color of tree bark, the dark burnt-red of the clinker brick of our family's house, and the differing greens of the elm and ash leaves. Barks, building materials and foliage are all elements to take on board when planning a scheme since in gardens, as in houses, we never see colors in isolation. A red-brick path, for

OPPOSITE The strong color—and tonal—contrast between the peach tints of burning bush and the pale green and the deep purple copper beech foliage is the chief focus here at Robin Hill, but bright green ferns, the slab of granite, the bleached stones of the Appian Way, and the white cupola of the little house built to amuse my young son, all contribute important elements to this colorfield picture. BELOW In spring, a circle of *Rhododendron* 'Coccineum Speciosum' lights up the woodland at Robin Hill.

instance, would clash with bright vermilion flowers; so if you want to keep the flowers, you might make the path of beige gravel or mown grass. At Robin Hill the exterior walls, and those that run through the garden, have been left a weathered white to harmonize with the subdued colors of the planting, and the blue-gray gravel was chosen to blend with the slate roof.

The colors of containers and pots need choosing with the same care that you would give to finding the right color for the toss pillows for a sofa, or the porcelain for a dining room. Terra-cotta, for example, is not anonymous; it contributes as much color to a scheme as any strong-hued flower.

Some of the most beautiful gardens are those with no flowers at all; but if foliage and manmade features take center stage, the choice of plants has to be very carefully made. Plants, like rooms, need contrast. But in the same way that juxtaposing various white paints can reveal the minute, yet significant, differences between them, so you will see that when you plant several different greens together some will appear almost black, others chartreuse. A mix of silver, purple, golden, and green leaves, especially when combined with variously shaped leaves, can make a richly rewarding tapestry.

SIGNATURE HOMES

The preceding chapters have outlined my design principles but, of course, they do not work in isolation from one another. The illustrations of homes that follow demonstrate that, like a composer, I try to use the principles to orchestrate a design symphony: at times, one principle is featured, while others play a supporting role; on other occasions, the principles appear to merge and are all but indistinguishable.

My sketch and a glimpse of the napping loggia at my house near Santa Barbara.

A Pacific Retreat

The Mediterranean climate has pulled me toward mid-California, like filings to a magnet, since I was sixteen years old. Finally I was fortunate enough to find a spot high up in the hills of Santa Barbara where I could make a sanctuary amid my own western Arcadia. The spectacular view of the harbor and sea, and the natural suroundings, are a joyful rationale for the colors that I used in both the house and the garden: shades of periwinkle blue, silver-gray, white, terra-cotta, and beige. The exterior stucco of the house is a dusky sandalwood color that is the exact shade of the bark of the eucalyptus trees that grow in the heavily wooded parts of my garden. Nearer the house a mix of solanum, rosemary, lavender, and gray santolina mingle happily under the canopies of umbrella pines, Portuguese cork oaks, and silver-gray olive trees. The same colors, especially the lavender blues, come indoors as upholstery, slipcovers, and tapestry fabrics; and the color of the terra-cotta tiles that cover all the outdoor terraces and indoor floors offsets the cooler colors and reminds me of the arid mountains that can be seen in the distance.

Looking across what is actually one huge room reveals three zones: the dining room, entry hall, and living room. The walls of the living room are painted soft putty gray-beige, all the other "rooms" are white. The terra-cotta floor tiles unify the indoor and outdoor spaces, contributing to the illusion that the house is a pavilion and also that it is larger than it is in reality.

BELOW LEFT The north–south axis leads from the motor court through the entry zone of the house. Partly an extension of the dining area, and partly an extension of the living room, this area is given added interest by the pale cream Oushak carpet, a pair of antique Continental chairs, and a collection of tomato-colored leather trunks and boxes stacked against the periwinkle-blue high-backed, slipcovered sofa.

BELOW CENTER The floor-to-ceiling 12-foot-high glass windows and doors turn the house into a vitrine so that the view seems to fill the living room. The comfortable furnishings were chosen for their simple geometric shapes, and the colors of the fabrics to be sympathetic with the flowers that tumble over the edge of the terrace. One of my signature touches is the picture that appears to be temporarily propped up on the mantelpiece rather than being hung permanently above it.

BELOW RIGHT The kitchen area, tucked into a corner of the ground floor, is largely veiled from view by a gray voile curtain. The cantilevered end of the heavy work-counter doubles as a table at which one can sit and eat.

BELOW A minimalist discipline was applied to the many planes of this corner of my bedroom. As in a painting by Mondrian, negative and positive spaces play an equal part, either as walls, windows, or the antique screen (see also page 120).

RIGHT A bust of Sir Francis Drake, the first English-speaking person to see the Pacific, now views the harbor of Santa Barbara from a corner of my bedroom. The modular, precision-hung views of the Roman Pantheon above the bed are softened by the bedspread, a romantic pastoral view of woodland in grisaille. Thus classical order is juxtaposed with romance.

The antique ruined column in my bathroom is placed so that it becomes the visual reward at the end of an axis. In addition, its imperfections and age make a sharp contrast to the uncompromising modernity of its setting. I hit upon the idea of hanging the shower curtains on lengths of rustproof chain so that steam can escape easily and the bathroom is kept airy.

The south-facing terrace, which runs the length of the main house, is paved with the same terra-cotta that is used indoors. The strictly linear, international style of the architecture of the house is offset by the romance of the tied-back drapery, the nineteenth-century French garden chairs, and the ornaments—the Turkish marble basin that acts as a bird bath and the green-patinated miniature urns on the table. I often like to introduce something fragile or perishable—in this case the drapery that moves in the wind—to contrast with, and thus exaggerate, the permanent, unyielding structure of the house. The setting unabashedly conjures up youthful memories of the movie sets of *Samson anad Delilah*.

LEFT A covered passageway, cooled and softened by climbing plants, leads to the guest house.

ABOVE LEFT AND RIGHT Made cozy by the presence of the fireplace, the simple living room and bedroom in the guest house also suggest a holiday escape. The British officer's canvas-and-leather campaign chairs are like old friends; they lived in my rooms when I was a student at Yale. The leather Shelter sofa, long a part of my own furniture collection, unfolds into a bed for extra guests.

The blue flowers of *Solanum rantonnetii* 'Grandiflorum', which are native to California, play at the feet of eucalyptus trees near the guest house, their trunks framing a miniature umbrella pine tree on the terrace. My enduring attachment to the ancient world is symbolized by this small potted tree; it reminds me of the huge, parent versions that surround the nymphaeum of Hadrian's Villa near Rome.

A New York Vitrine

This apartment was bought as a *pied-à-terre* by a couple who had social and business interests in New York City. Like so many apartments that are not the occupants' chief residence, the second bedroom had to do triple duty— as a room for the couple's young children when they were in the city, for occasional guests, and as a home office. The initial appeal of this otherwise featureless flat was its floor-to-ceiling glass windows with their staggering views of Central Park. So my aim was to transform a series of boxes in a single drawer of what I call "a filing cabinet for the living" into backgrounds that were equal to the view.

By moving walls and concealing doors, I made a large L-shaped living room that makes the best use of a corner with two walls of glass. To fully exploit the effect of this light-filled space, I hung the entrance foyer with murky, teal-colored fabric to create a softly enveloping tunnel (and hide unattractive closet doors). This enclosure causes visitors to pause, subliminally wiping their visual slates clean, and propels them toward the light ahead. Once they are released into that space, they perceive it as larger and lighter by comparison with the small, dark entrance.

The end of the living room is furnished sparingly but exquisitely as an entrance hallway to suggest space and grandeur. The visitor's first view, from the foyer, is framed by two seventeenth-century Italian baroque serpentine columns. Concealed in the wall at the far end is a door that opens into the kitchen.

Looking back from the windows in the living room shows how the focal point, the ruined eighteenth-century French mirror, has been emphasized both by the flanking doors and by the paneled archway. The vertical ornament, an antique piece of forged iron fretwork, on the wall to the right has been placed there to balance the narrower width of the wall opposite. The soft, linen-covered walls and exaggerated cornice temper the severity of the modern proportions of the rooms, while the sofa is upholstered in the same fabric as the walls in order to maximize the feeling of space. The folding screen (*below*) conceals a large television set and also helps to give a more intimate, cozy feeling to this end of the room. Here you could retreat and curl up with a book away from the sometimes overpoweringly dazzling view.

The substantial, weight-bearing support in the corner of the living room has been visually dissolved by cladding it with mirrors and continuing the woodwork of the windows to the right and left of it. A third wall to the left (not seen), is also mirrored and the same molding used again, to replicate the effect of real windows. The result makes visitors believe that they are seated in the middle of a vitrine with uninterrupted, 180-degree views. The large crown molding conceals sources of soft lighting so there are no lamps to create disturbing reflections in the windows after dark. The carpet organizes the conversation area and separates it from the dining space.

The twin beds in the second bedroom are furnished as sofas in the daytime so that the space can be used as an office. The deep red accents—the color of old, handmade bricks—were used to give the room an atmosphere that would appeal to the young children who use it on the occasions when they are in New York.

The doors, which, like all the doors in the apartment, were standard flat metal plates, have been disguised by classical molding and paintwork.

The queen-size bed in the master bedroom was custom-designed to stand high above the floor. This creates the illusion of more space because it allows a greater area of carpet to be visible than a traditional bed which, with its skirting to the ground, would have seemed to fill up the narrow room. The armoire opposite the bed was also custom-designed: the top conceals uplighting, the doors slide back into pockets to reveal the television, and the drawers below provide much-needed storage. In order not to shroud the effect of the vitrine, heavy drapes have been banished in favor of light blinds.

A Hampton Long House

This house, which I designed and built, sits high on a sand dune at the end of Long Island, overlooking the Atlantic Ocean. Taking inspiration from the vernacular architecture of early eighteenth-century farmers, I conceived a rambling dwelling to suggest that several generations had lived here and, as they prospered, had added on to the original structure. Some of the barn-like buildings are based on what are known as "colonial salt boxes" after the shape of the roofs, which slope further toward the ground on one side than the other in order to cover a lower-height extension; one section is a two-story octagonal tower that looks like the remains of a lighthouse. Although the building has a timber frame, I took the liberty of using old brick, instead of the wood normally found in the locale, for most of the outside walls except for those of the guest wing, which is clad in cedar shingle. The use of different materials—bricks, shingles, and hand-split wooden roofing shingles—supports the concept of the house as an accretion of additions over a long time, and visually helps to break down the scale of what is very large residence.

Emphasized by exposing the timber post-and-beam construction, the scale of the interior public spaces is more agricultural than domestic. The impression of a venerable old barn is increased in the living room by the stone floors, scratch-coat plaster walls, and hand-hewn beams. The room has been left deliberately underfurnished so that in winter the focus is the huge fireplace, and in summer it is the immense glazed doors that open up to uninterrupted views of the sea (see page 170).

BELOW The driveway leads up to the motor court, and to the front of the house, which has two entrances: the great front doors in the central, rectangular section of the building, and the porticoed family entrance that leads into the octagonal tower on the left. This building contains the wine cellar, the library, and the master bedroom, stacked on top of one another. The triangular window shown on page 80 can be seen in the apex of the pitched roof of the central section; the guest wing extends further to the right of this.

RIGHT Broad, ramped stairs lead to the great front doors. These are opened for guests and during warm weather. A small door that is cut into the big one, a design based on the west doors of the great European cathedrals, is used more frequently. There are matching doors in the opposite wall, and when both sets are open the effect is a *coup de théâtre*, a triumphal archway. This also allows views toward all four cardinal points—north, south, east, and west—from the entrance hall.

The plan of the main part of the house is a U shape round a central courtyard, the fourth side of which is open to the sea. The living-room windows are seen open (*left*) and closed (*above*). The vine-covered dining arbor and the outdoor fireplace (*right and right above*) give human scale to the generous proportions of the stone-paved entertaining terrace. The stainless-steel table stays out all year round, but the 2-foot-square blue ceramic tiles can be lifted and brought inside for the cold months.

LEFT The kitchen is divided into three areas: for cooking, for eating, and, in the foreground, for sitting round the fire. The cooking area, containing all the appliances, counters, and cooking surfaces, is enclosed in a snug inglenook—which is tucked under the eaves of one of the "salt box" roofs. Strong work-light is directed on to the counters, leaving gentler, ambient light to make the most of the open rafters in the eating area.

RIGHT The entrance hall is to one side of the great front doors, and looks through to the dining room. The thin, hand-forged iron balustrade is like a ribbon that guides the occupants up to the floor above.

BELOW The formal dining room, with its smooth plaster walls and polished joinery, is more finished than the rest of the house, yet retains its simple, primitive feel. The wooden chair and chest, rare pieces of seventeenth-century "pilgrim" American furniture, mingle with chairs, a table, and a lamp from my own collection. A minimalist concern for serenity persuaded me to leave the walls unadorned; and wanting to suggest that the room was more like a drawing than a completed painting prompted me to leave the picture propped up on the chest.

RIGHT In the octagonal master bedroom, sev___ ___f French doors open to sweeping views of the Atlan___ ___g Island farm fields. The Shaker-style canopy bed is exac___ ___me width as the passage that leads to the bedroom; the char___ ___he passage is a genuine Shaker piece. A nineteenth-century garden gate hangs on the wall like a modern painting. The tour de force is a collection of tiny seventeenth-century courting mirrors (given by suitors, treasured by recipients) which help to force the perspective, making the far wall appear to be further away than it really is.

LEFT The upstairs sitting room, used primarily for reading and letter writing, duplicates the simplicity of the dining room directly below it. The sofa and chaise from my collection are modern neighbors to the eighteenth-century American painted table and the Connecticut spindle-back Windsor chair.

RIGHT Nestling in the chaise is what is perhaps one of my best-known signature details: a rolled-up quilt making an armrest or pillow. It is, in a sense, a fragment of my youth— it harks back to my student days when I entertained fantasies of being a cowboy and sleeping on a bedroll!

LEFT A freestanding vanity in the middle of a guest bathroom stands just above the sunken shower floor. This bathroom challenges most people's expectations of privacy. It is almost an adjunct to the garden: when the French doors are open visitors feel that they are showering outdoors and toweling off inches away from a path that leads to the Atlantic.

RIGHT The powder room immediately to the right of the great front doors continues the theme of hand-hewn craftsmanship: a huge wooden lintel has been carved into a sink, the tiles are handmade, and the iron mirror-frame was forged by a blacksmith. The sinuously curving pewter swan's head faucet provides a frisson of surprise, its polished sophistication momentarily seeming to belong to a different aesthetic canon.

A City Coach House

When the time came for me to downsize from my large apartment in New York, I looked at about forty penthouses before coming upon a nineteenth-century coach house on two floors with a small, urban garden. The street was charming, as was the façade, and I had always wanted a garden in the city; and although the interior was a maze of small, depressingly dark rooms, I saw how I could open it up and let in light from both sides of the house. When I reconfigured the space, I put the major rooms on the outsides of the house and sandwiched the service areas between them, but squeezed these to the sides so that it became possible to see through the house from front to back. The rich cinnabar color of the brick walls, most of which had been left exposed, appealed to me and was the touchstone for the color palette. This ranged from espresso to beige, through shades of bronze and amethyst, set off by white. For accent, I included touches of magenta, like the silk of a cardinal's robe.

I canopied the brick-floored garden with white raincoat fabric to edit out the urban chaos above it; made a pool to provide the sound of moving water; and, among a throng of potted plants, I included ferns, four fastigiate maples, and a succession of white flowers from early hyacinths to 'Casablanca' lilies.

I upholstered the walls and ceiling of the guest room in natural linen, making it acoustically and visually calm. A stack of humble wooden garden flats separates a worn, eighteenth-century Italian leather chair and the sensual collection of cushions on the day bed.

LEFT In designing the guest room, I intentionally left the linen-upholstered walls largely unadorned to give the room a sense of serenity, so that it could become an oasis for the urban traveler. The furniture includes an antique mercury-mirror and an Italian desk and chairs. The attentuated Tube lamp is one of the range from my collection, as is the ottoman which is quilted in wool recycled from house-movers' blankets.

RIGHT The linen-draped dressing room with its small Napoleonic campaign chairs suggests an officer's tent. It is a handsome, poor man's alternative to a wood-paneled fitted dressing room. The pole in the middle of the room is the hot-water pipe that rises through the building. I use it to warm the bath towels—hence the hooks.

LEFT A table top is an inviting opportunity to make a still life. Here a collection of eighteenth-century manganese Delftware, Chinese vases, rare snuff boxes, a carved eighteenth-century sleeping lion, a French olive-storage jar, and pink ranunculi stand on a Louis XIII table. Missing from this vignette is my *petit point* pillow that claims "Inner peace through possessions"!

BELOW The contrast of the supple leather headboard and plush velvet bedspread with the abrasive brick wall, and the eclectic mix of furniture, which includes an eighteenth-century English tea table and a Louis XIII farm table as well as one of my own bronze-and-glass book tables, are examples of my penchant for juxtaposing opposites—soft with hard, rare with found, old with new.

In the living room, the amethyst-white ceiling and plastered walls, the high-gloss lacquered ceiling molding, and the shimmering cotton slipcovers are a smooth foil for the rough, catacomb-like brick walls, which I wanted to celebrate almost as though an archaeological dig had unearthed an earlier surface.

The bronze silk-velvet-covered sofa looks as if it was made as a companion to the minimalist colorfield painting by Power Booth. In fact it was a happy coincidence: the Club sofa, the first of my sofas in production (and which is still in production), fitted perfectly. In keeping with my belief that in a modest space the largest piece of furniture in a room should be the color of either the walls or of the floor, the two largest elements here—the sofa and the painting—meld into the dark brick walls.

A Villa Apartment

This family-sized apartment in one of the Upper East Side buildings of Manhattan feels more like a villa when one is inside it. It belongs to European clients, who spend the winter months in America and the summer at home by the Mediterranean. They wanted a classically elegant apartment in which they could entertain with ease, and display their collection of modern paintings and Greek and Roman sculpture, and which the whole family could use as their New York base—the older children are at university in America, the younger children are not yet old enough to go to school. Involving major construction and complicated electronic technology, the remodeling took a considerable time and was still in the process of being finished when these photographs were taken.

The apartment clearly reveals my three-sided inclinations. It combines romantically corroded, or rich, surfaces with an almost Zen-like obsession with minimalism and a vocabulary of architectural classicism.

The view from the bedroom corridor toward the entrance hall has a Hellenic torso as the focal point. The pair of Doric columns supports a dropped ceiling that psychologically separates the foyer and makes a secondary vestibule which canopies the double doors that lead into the drawing room. This also physically conceals electrical and air-conditioning ducts.

ABOVE AND RIGHT These two views of the entrance hall, looking in opposite directions, both have a central focus: the antique carved wooden sea shell above the fireplace, and the pediment-topped double doors. The restrained classical detailing and proportions of the hallway make more of an impact because they are offset by the unexpectedly humble

textural impact of the unfinished-looking scratch-coat plaster and the newly carved stone chimneypiece, which suggest that this room was conceived as partly an outdoor space and partly an indoor one. The furnishings are minimal, yet there is a touch of romantic extravagance about the cut-velvet brocade that drapes the side table.

In the dining room I placed a small breakfast table at the window—as I do in most large dining rooms—so that if only two people are eating here they do not feel Marion Davies and William Randolph Hearst at either end of a vast dining table.

I designed a huge cornice and entablature, finished in glossy lacquer and embellished with oxidized silver leafing, to control the monumental scale of the room; I added residential scale with the eighteenth-century painted canvas Italian panel that leans against the wall, framing it with a pair of plaster-cast urns; and I introduced the third, human, scale with the folding purple silk-covered screen. This screen, which does double duty by concealing the television, is reversible: the other side is covered with bleached horsehair so that when the slipcovers and china are changed from one season to another, it can be turned round to be unobtrusively neutral.

The walls are upholstered, in celadon-colored silk, which makes acoustic compensation for the decision not to have a carpet. The same fabric lines the platinum-colored Peking-silk-velvet curtains.

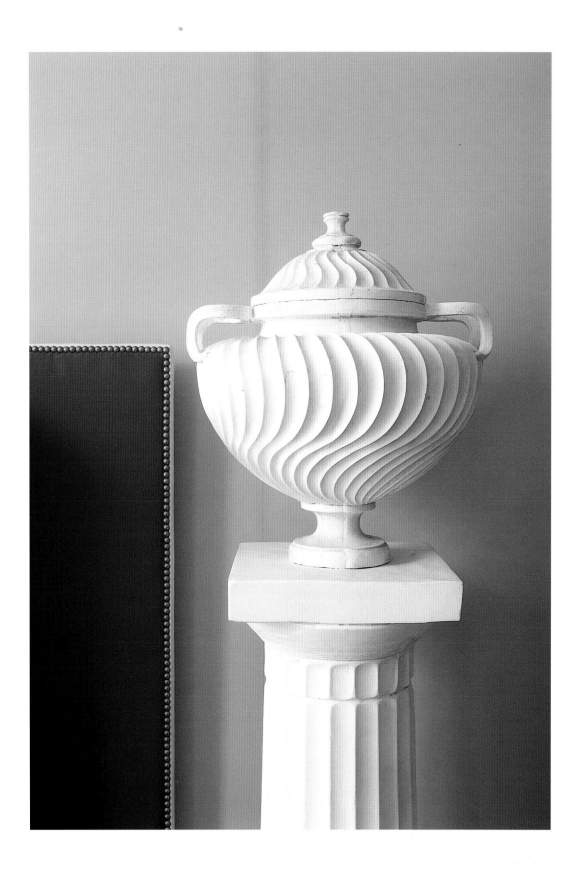

I made the dining room square, so that it could accommodate four separate round tables for large parties. When this happens, the chandelier, with its alabaster shades, is disconnected, leaving the ceiling downlights, sideboard lamps, and numerous candles to provide the lighting. (The plaster ceiling-rose is also the source of the air conditioning.) The leather slipcovered dining chairs from my collection, on casters, are neutral enough to sit next to the extra folding chairs that are hidden by the damask-covered sideboards. The ornament over the chimneypiece is a classical urn cut from worn roofing tin. Like an unsophisticated, weather-beaten country cousin who has come to dine among soigné company in a city room, its ravaged face stands out amid the shimmering silk and polished silver.

LEFT The eighteenth-century French *boiserie* was probably installed in the drawing room in the 1930s. It was the only room the proportions of which I did not alter. However, to give it a more youthful ambience, I bleached the paneling, pickled the hardwood floors so that they became a light silver-gray, and used mostly cool-colored fabrics. The furnishings, mostly from my own furniture collection, meld equally well with contemporary or period decoration.

RIGHT What appear to be shelves of antique books are actually only a veneer: the book spines on molding conceal doors that cover the stereo cabinet and bar. Next to them is a glimpse of the leather-wrapped doors with oxidized bronze studs that open into the drawing room. During a large party they can be folded back flush into recesses.

The cool colors, minimal furnishings, and lack of extraneous detail in the master bedroom make it a sanctuary where one can get away from the jangle, bustle, and detritus of the day. The walls are the faintest shade of blue; the ceiling is custom-made wallpaper that was airbrushed from smoky-green edges into celadon and then into icy-white in the center. The lounge chair and ottoman, the desk and the lamp, all from my collection, are anonymous enough not to deflect attention from the classical moldings and the sense of serenity that pervades this nurturing, yet liberating, space.

Subtle halogen downlights in the window recesses give the bedroom a gentle glow at
night, while paper shades at the windows can be pulled up from the bottom to provide as
much privacy as is needed. I have always contrived to hide technical details, such as
lighting, heating, ventilation, and humidifying ducts: in this apartment they are concealed
in an undetectable space between the crown moldings and the ceilings. I also feel that the
stereo, and especially the television, should be out of sight when not in use. Here they are
housed in a pair of custom-made cabinets (one is seen below).

The master bathroom, with its marble walls and luxurious large marble double-sink vanity, is like an imperial spa room—the marble and mosaic floor and oval bathtub have more to do with Roman Pompeii than twenty-first-century New York.

A room like this delivers far more than the means for physical refreshment; in fulfilling sybaritic dreams, it offers balm for the soul.

LEFT A Roman senator might feel at home, grilling his enemies, under the Pantheon-like floating wooden coffered ceiling of the kitchen. He would have been familiar, too, with most of the materials used here: granite, wood, and stone. The dark shade of teal on the lower cabinets was used to be sympathetic with the color of the granite, while the upper cabinets duplicate the greige color of the wooden coffers.

RIGHT This powder room is actually two spaces. The vestibule has a seating banquette on the left and a console supported by early twentieth-century sea horses on the right, and acts more as a small withdrawing room. Through the platinum velvet portières is the lavatory where the silver travertine volcanic-stone walls have been left natural and unpolished. Even a short axis can be made into a dramatic statement by being given a focus: here a niche, underscored by a sweepingly simple stool, is decorated with a single, perfect flower.

EPILOGUE

M ORE LIKE A DRAWING than a finished picture, what I call the napping loggia in my home in California (*opposite*) illustrates how my design principles apply to the humblest of spaces. Even here, an axis has been created, using symmetry, and offers a glimpse through the tiny portal as the finale of the visual journey. The scale ranges from the massive trellis overhead to the intimate double chaise; a theatrical element of surprise is seen in the indoor/outdoor conundrum and in the contrast of luxury with simplicity. The everchanging play of light and shadow, through the day and the seasons, speaks for itself. (At night the loggia is lit by flickering candles.) The colors—the nuanced, watered-down blue paint on the wall of old boards, the weathered silvery patina on the beams overhead, and the pale beige of the carpet—are all echoes of, and therefore are in harmony with, the natural colors that surround the loggia.

I like to think of the napping loggia as a spiritual sibling to the Boscoreale sleeping chamber excavated near Pompeii and now displayed at the Metropolitan Museum of Art in New York. To view the bedchamber is to marvel at the hand of an ancient conjurer. The vaulted ceiling, *trompe l'oeil* cornices, and architectural columns push back the confines of the six planes, rearranging our perceptions of space in this 10-foot-wide room. But illusion has created something beyond a prosaic bedroom: it is a ceremonial sleeping chamber. The mosaic floor becomes a carpet; the footstool makes a major comment as it leads to the bed, which is raised on a platform, evoking an altar to be approached for the luxury of sleep.

Both the Boscoreale bedchamber and the napping loggia are rooms that provide far more than basic shelter. Both offer the emotional comfort of a cocoon. Both play games with physical space: at Pompeii the walls portray the open sky whereas in the loggia the ceiling is open to the actual sky. In both, the simplest objects are revered and nothing is superfluous.

The combination of security and of unfettered, unencumbered space can release us from, and elevate us above, the distractions of everyday life. This feeling of protection and the possibility of a fleeting moment of transcendence is what I believe interior design should be all about, and what I continually strive to create.

LEFT The sleeping chamber of the Villa P. Fannius Synistor from Boscoreale, which is approximately a mile north of Pompeii, is a room with more imagined than actual space. Though the couch and footstool come from other Roman villas of later date, the walls and ceiling were painted in the first century BC.

LEFT The napping loggia at my Pacific hideway near Santa Barbara was created from an old carport. Serene and comfortable, it is an invitation to escape— at least for a while— from the pressures of everyday life.

INDEX

———

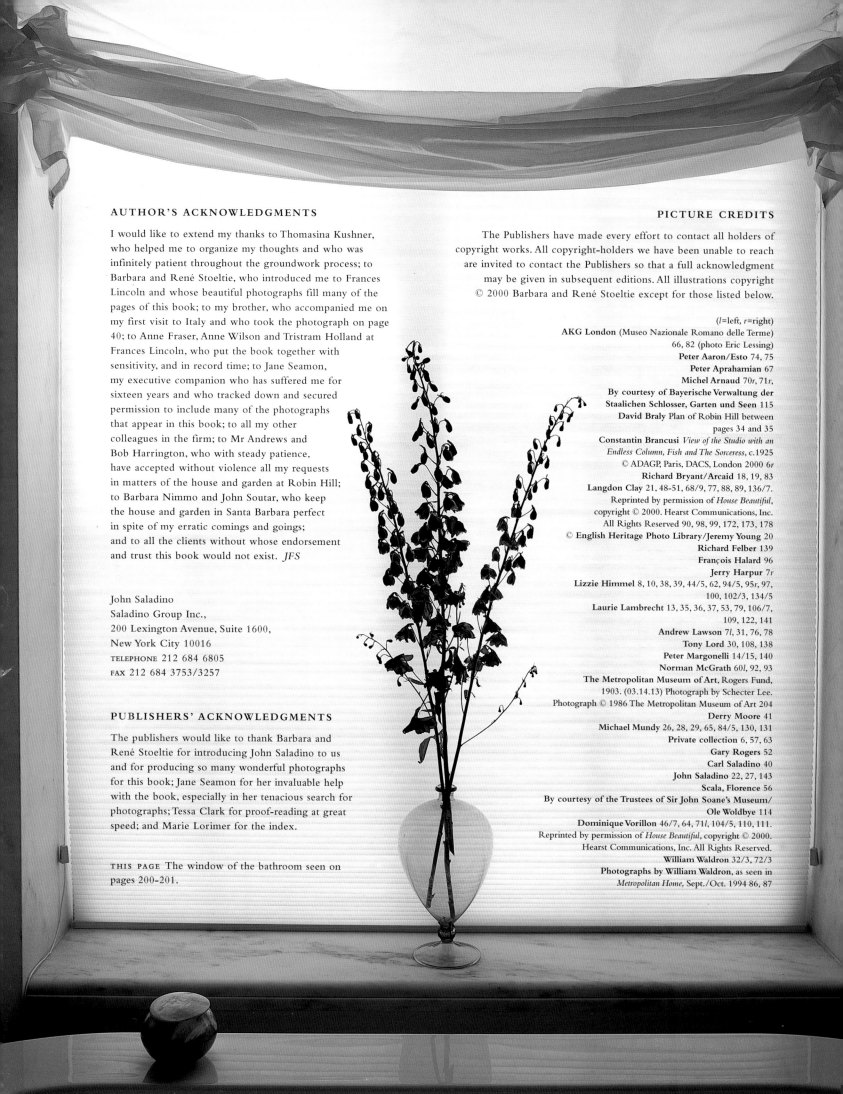

AUTHOR'S ACKNOWLEDGMENTS

I would like to extend my thanks to Thomasina Kushner, who helped me to organize my thoughts and who was infinitely patient throughout the groundwork process; to Barbara and René Stoeltie, who introduced me to Frances Lincoln and whose beautiful photographs fill many of the pages of this book; to my brother, who accompanied me on my first visit to Italy and who took the photograph on page 40; to Anne Fraser, Anne Wilson and Tristram Holland at Frances Lincoln, who put the book together with sensitivity, and in record time; to Jane Seamon, my executive companion who has suffered me for sixteen years and who tracked down and secured permission to include many of the photographs that appear in this book; to all my other colleagues in the firm; to Mr Andrews and Bob Harrington, who with steady patience, have accepted without violence all my requests in matters of the house and garden at Robin Hill; to Barbara Nimmo and John Soutar, who keep the house and garden in Santa Barbara perfect in spite of my erratic comings and goings; and to all the clients without whose endorsement and trust this book would not exist. *JFS*

John Saladino
Saladino Group Inc.,
200 Lexington Avenue, Suite 1600,
New York City 10016
TELEPHONE 212 684 6805
FAX 212 684 3753/3257

PUBLISHERS' ACKNOWLEDGMENTS

The publishers would like to thank Barbara and René Stoeltie for introducing John Saladino to us and for producing so many wonderful photographs for this book; Jane Seamon for her invaluable help with the book, especially in her tenacious search for photographs; Tessa Clark for proof-reading at great speed; and Marie Lorimer for the index.

THIS PAGE The window of the bathroom seen on pages 200-201.

PICTURE CREDITS

The Publishers have made every effort to contact all holders of copyright works. All copyright-holders we have been unable to reach are invited to contact the Publishers so that a full acknowledgment may be given in subsequent editions. All illustrations copyright © 2000 Barbara and René Stoeltie except for those listed below.

(*l*=left, *r*=right)
AKG London (Museo Nazionale Romano delle Terme) 66, 82 (photo Eric Lessing)
Peter Aaron/Esto 74, 75
Peter Aprahamian 67
Michel Arnaud 70*r*, 71*r*,
By courtesy of Bayerische Verwaltung der Staalichen Schlosser, Garten und Seen 115
David Braly Plan of Robin Hill between pages 34 and 35
Constantin Brancusi *View of the Studio with an Endless Column, Fish and The Sorceress*, c.1925 © ADAGP, Paris, DACS, London 2000 6*r*
Richard Bryant/Arcaid 18, 19, 83
Langdon Clay 21, 48-51, 68/9, 77, 88, 89, 136/7. Reprinted by permission of *House Beautiful*, copyright © 2000. Hearst Communications, Inc. All Rights Reserved 90, 98, 99, 172, 173, 178
© English Heritage Photo Library/Jeremy Young 20
Richard Felber 139
François Halard 96
Jerry Harpur 7*r*
Lizzie Himmel 8, 10, 38, 39, 44/5, 62, 94/5, 95*r*, 97, 100, 102/3, 134/5
Laurie Lambrecht 13, 35, 36, 37, 53, 79, 106/7, 109, 122, 141
Andrew Lawson 7*l*, 31, 76, 78
Tony Lord 30, 108, 138
Peter Margonelli 14/15, 140
Norman McGrath 60*l*, 92, 93
The Metropolitan Museum of Art, Rogers Fund, 1903. (03.14.13) Photograph by Schecter Lee. Photograph © 1986 The Metropolitan Museum of Art 204
Derry Moore 41
Michael Mundy 26, 28, 29, 65, 84/5, 130, 131
Private collection 6, 57, 63
Gary Rogers 52
Carl Saladino 40
John Saladino 22, 27, 143
Scala, Florence 56
By courtesy of the Trustees of Sir John Soane's Museum/ Ole Woldbye 114
Dominique Vorillon 46/7, 64, 71*l*, 104/5, 110, 111. Reprinted by permission of *House Beautiful*, copyright © 2000. Hearst Communications, Inc. All Rights Reserved.
William Waldron 32/3, 72/3
Photographs by William Waldron, as seen in *Metropolitan Home*, Sept./Oct. 1994 86, 87